Managing
Management
Climate

George G. Gordon
Hay Associates

Walter Cummins
Fairleigh Dickinson University

Lexington Books
D.C. Heath and Company
Lexington, Massachusetts
Toronto

Library of Congress Cataloging in Publication Data

Gordon, George G.
    Managing management climate.

    Includes index.
    1. Management. I. Cummins, Walter M., joint author. II. Title. III. Title:
Management climate.
HD38.G629   658.4   78-19615
ISBN 0-669-02545-3

Copyright © 1979 by D.C. Heath and Company

Published simultaneously in Canada

Printed in the United States of America

International Standard Book Number: 0-669-02545-3

Library of Congress Catalog Card Number: 78-19615

To Janet

Contents

List of Figures   xi

List of Tables   xv

Preface   xvii

Acknowledgments   xix

Part I   *Understanding Climate*   1

Chapter 1   **The Role of Climate in Enterprise Management**   3

Typical Explanations of Success   3
The Nature of Climate   4
Climate and Success   5
Attitude Surveys Versus Climate Analysis   9
Complexity of Climate   10

Chapter 2   **Antecedents of Climate**   11

External Forces   11
Organizational History   13
The Role of Management   13

Chapter 3   **Communication and Motivation**   17

Communication of Intended Climate   17
Motivations and Perceptions   18
Upward Communication   19
Actual Versus Perceived Pay Practices   20

Part II   *Evaluating Climate*   23

Chapter 4   **Climate Measurement**   25

Two Perspectives of Climate   25
An Approach to Measuring Climate   27
Eight Climate Dimensions   29

Chapter 5   **Understanding the Dimensions of Climate**   33

Organizational Clarity   33
Decision-Making   34

Organizational Integration   35
Management Style   36
Performance Orientation   37
Organizational Vitality   38
Compensation   39
Human Resource Development   40
Other Climate Dimensions   40

Chapter 6   **Interpreting Climate Results**   41

Company Profiles—Alpha Corporation   42
Summary   53

Chapter 7   **Climate Trends Within an Organization**   55

Results by Management Levels   55
Results by Organizational Units   56
Staff-Line Differences   57

Chapter 8   **The "Right" Climate**   61

Climate Relationships Among Organizations   61
Climate and Results   63
Climate, Morale, and Performance Demand   64
Climate Ratings and Organizational Differences   67
Industry Profiles   70
Job Security   75
Organization Size   79
Capital Intensity   79
Stages of Business Development   80

Part III   *Managing Climate*   85

Chapter 9   **Strategy and Planning**   87

Redirecting Management Processes—Cargo
     Shipping Company   87
Capability for Goal-Setting and Strategic
     Planning—Equipment Manufacturing Company   91
Strategy Recommendations—Thermal Gas
     Company   95
Marketing Strategy—Magnum Foods   98

Chapter 10   **Organizational Restructuring**   103

Restructuring to Increase Sales Volume and
     Profitability—Driver Corporation   103

Restructuring of a Service Organization—the
  Agency   112
Restructuring for New Product Development—
  Clerical Equipment Company   115

Chapter 11   **Rewards and Motivation**   121

Climate and Overall Management Compensation—
  Bluestone Mining   121
Compensation and Motivation—Spencer-Huxley
  Company   126
Creating an Incentive Program—Kingsley
  Insurance   129
Perceptions of Benefits—Kelly-Landor
  Corporation   133
Sales Incentives—Hazlitt Corporation   135
Motivating and Developing Key Staff Managers—
  United Diversity   141

Chapter 12   **Manpower Development**   147

Failures of the Existing System   147
Objectives and Critical Areas for Change   148
Role of Climate Analysis   150

Chapter 13   **Management by Objectives**   153

Climate Issues   154
Implementing Management by Objectives   157

Chapter 14   **External Influences**   159

Market Images of an Engine Manufacturer   159
Introducing a New Banking Service   162

Chapter 15   **Effective Climate Management**   165

Action-Oriented Problem-Solving   166
The Commitment to Change   168
Monitoring Climate Over Time   169
Translating Issues to Action   172
Options for Management   172
Climate Analysis—the Management Tool of
  the Future   174

Appendix A   A Word About Causality   175

Appendix B   Items Included in Each of the Climate
                 Dimensions   177

                 Index   179

                 About the Authors   185

List of Figures

4-1	A Model of Organizational Functioning	26
4-2	Questions in the Performance Orientation Dimension	30
4-3	Graphic Presentation of Dimension Results	31
4-4	Graphic Presentation of Item Results	32
6-1	Alpha Corporation—Overall Company Results	43
6-2	Alpha Corporation—Results by Reporting Level	44
6-3	Alpha Corporation—Organizational Clarity	45
6-4	Alpha Corporation—Decision-Making	46
6-5	Alpha Corporation—Organizational Integration	47
6-6	Alpha Corporation—Management Style	48
6-7	Alpha Corporation—Performance Orientation	49
6-8	Alpha Corporation—Organizational Vitality	50
6-9	Alpha Corporation—Compensation	51
6-10	Alpha Corporation—Human Resource Development	52
7-1	An Example of Similar Profiles with a Gap Between Top Management and Other Reporting Levels	56
7-2	An Example of Dissimilar Profiles Between Management Levels	57
7-3	An Example of Similar Profiles for Two Operating Divisions in the Same Company	58
7-4	An Example of Dissimilar Profiles for Three Operating Divisions in the Same Company	59
7-5	Climate Profiles for Line and Staff Groups	60
8-1	Correlations of Climate Profiles Between and Within Companies	62
8-2	Correlations Between Climate Dimensions and Five-Year Growth in Net Profit	64
8-3	Comparison of Two Company Profiles	68

8-4	Company B—Management Style Results	69
8-5	Industry Profiles	72
8-6	Utility Scores on Integration and Clarity	74
8-7	Utility Scores on Management of Human Resources	75
8-8	Perceived Job Security by Industry	76
8-9	Climate Profiles for Different Security Patterns	77
8-10	Business Assessment Matrix	81
8-11	Organization Assessment Matrix	83
9-1	Cargo Shipping Company—Information Basis for Marketing Planning	89
9-2	Cargo Shipping Company—Marketing Vitality	90
9-3	Equipment Manufacturing Company—Extent of Planning Effectiveness by Area	92
9-4	Equipment Manufacturing Company—Quality of Accounting Systems Information	93
9-5	Thermal Gas Company—Actual and Desired Emphasis on Various Business Objectives	96
9-6	Magnum Foods—Preferred Focus of Business Development Efforts	99
9-7	Magnum Foods—Clarity of Direction	100
10-1	Driver Corporation—Overall Company Results	105
10-2	Driver Corporation—Unit Results	106
10-3	Driver Corporation—Major Perceived Factors That Hinder Sales	107
10-4	Driver Corporation—Proposed Organization of the Marketing Division	109
10-5	Driver Corporation—Sections of the Implementation Plan Chart	111
10-6	Clerical Equipment Company—Indicators of Integration Problems	118
10-7	Clerical Equipment Company—Problems of Human Resource Management	119

11-1   Bluestone Mining—Opinions of Compensation and
        Salary Administration   125

11-2   Spencer-Huxley—Comparison of Personal Motivation
        and Management Climate   127

11-3   Kingsley Insurance Company—Differences Between
        Existing and Desired Security   131

11-4   Kelly-Landor Corporation—Characterization of the
        Current Bonus Plan   134

11-5   Kelly-Landor Corporation—Perceived Benefit Value
        Analysis   136

11-6   Hazlitt Corporation—Current Compensation
        Program   139

11-7   United Diversity—Criteria for Identification of a
        Top-Level Specialist   142

11-8   United Diversity—Percentage of Each Group Oriented
        Toward Higher- and Lower-Order Needs   144

12-1   American Distributing—Changes in Perceptions and
        Performance   152

13-1   Zenith Distributing—Climate and Productivity in
        Two Locations   155

14-1   Burlingham Engine Company—Executive Impressions
        of Customer Images   160

14-2   Burlingham Engine Company—Competitive Image
        From Three Perspectives   162

14-3   Burlingham Engine Company—Comparison of the
        Three Major Companies on Delivery Time   163

List of Tables

8-1	Climate Items Most Related to Demand and Satisfaction	65
9-1	Percent of Time Spent in Short-, Medium-, or Long-Term Planning: Equipment Manufacturing Company	92
11-1	Percentage of Respondents Indicating That Current Benefit Programs Do Not Meet Their Needs: Kelly-Landor Corporation	133
11-2	Comments on Rationale for Differential Assignment of Commissions: Hazlitt Corporation (Industrial Division)	140
12-1	Attitudes Toward Future Career Opportunities: American Distributing	151
12-2	Attitudes Toward the Type of Actions Required for Future Advancement: American Distributing	151
14-1	Agreement in Attitudes Toward Automated Banking	163

Preface

This book provides a comprehensive introduction to climate and its role in creative management. It is divided into three major parts, designed to help the reader understand the nature of climate, its measurement, and its use as a management tool to improve performance.

The first section, "Understanding Climate," explains the place of climate in an organization and how it develops. Part II, "Evaluating Climate," describes our methodology for measuring climate, interpreting the results of climate surveys, and developing comparative information about climate.

The third and longest section, "Managing Climate," reports on managerial applications of climate information by describing actual case studies, selected from the hundreds in our files. Although the names of the companies discussed are fictitious and their businesses are disguised to protect confidentiality, the vital information in each example—the company's situation, the purpose of the climate analysis, the findings of that analysis, and the actions resulting from those findings—is factual. The examples demonstrate the essential role that climate analysis has played in developing business strategies, plans for organizational restructuring, manpower development programs, and compensation programs. These case studies are by no means exhaustive. They indicate the range of applications that have already been accomplished and imply an even greater potential.

The book is directed toward two main audiences, line executives and personnel officers. Line executives will find the section on managing climate most instructive because it tells of practical applications made by others which may be appropriate for similar situations within their own companies. Personnel officers, who often have the responsibility for the actual implementation of a climate analysis, will, in addition to the applications in part III, find useful material on measurement and interpretation in the first two parts.

Acknowledgements

The problems described in this book are real problems, extracted from personal consulting experiences, memos, position papers, and reports to clients. We wish to express our appreciation to Hay Associates for making this material available to us. Because Hay is a major management consulting firm, its resources have afforded us the opportunity to obtain an in-depth knowledge of many of the most important companies in America.

We especially wish to thank the many professionals at Hay Associates whose consulting activities have made this book possible. Our thanks go to Roy Delizia, Neal Gelfand, Bonnie Goldberg, Marlene Goodison, James Gouthro, Ronald Grey, Michael Halbert, Robert Kosobud, Robert Muschewske, Charles Nesbitt, Avner Porat, Edward Ryterband, Arnold Silverman, Harold Smolinsky, Franco Vicino, and Martin Wolf. Finally, we are grateful to Howard Asofsky, Gerald Crane, and Edwin Hartman for their many helpful comments on the manuscript.

Part I
Understanding Climate

1 The Role of Climate in Enterprise Management

What makes a company successful? This may be the most frequently asked and yet inadequately answered question in business. Although the management literature is replete with definitive statements of why some companies are successful and others are not, no single, simple explanation exists. If it did, all companies would have the same set of tactics—the one that produces success.

Typical Explanations of Success

Market position, an outstanding executive leader, product strategies, and even fortuitous events are some typical explanations for success. But can it really be shown that any one of these factors is the key? Let us focus upon a single industry and see how these factors have operated. The tobacco industry provides an excellent example because it has a relatively limited line of products, a small number of participants, enough external influences to provide a significant challenge to management, and considerable volatility, reflected in dramatic changes in market positions.

In 1960 the tobacco industry was led by two companies, R.J. Reynolds and American Tobacco, which between them accounted for about 59 percent of the total sales. The other four major companies, Brown & Williamson, Philip Morris, P. Lorillard, and Liggett & Myers, each had between 9 and 12 percent of the market. By 1976 this picture had changed radically. At that time R.J. Reynolds held its share at 33 percent, while Philip Morris was in second place with 25 percent. Brown & Williamson had risen to about 16 percent, while American Tobacco had slipped from 26 to 14 percent of the market, a very dramatic slide when one considers that each percentage of market share is worth about $50 million in sales. Obviously, in the sixteen years covered there were some very clear "winners" and "losers" in the tobacco industry.

What factors triggered these gains and losses? At one time or another, the business press cited each of the four factors mentioned above, but a close examination of each reveals many contradictions. For instance:

Market Position—American Tobacco had a very strong market position in 1960; in fact, before 1958 it was the leading company in the industry. Yet by 1976 it had only 14 percent of the market.

Product Strategies—R.J. Reynolds, the current industry leader, has an announced strategy of producing a "brand in every growing or potential cigarette category" and frequently creates new brands for highly differentiated market segments.[1] Yet Philip Morris, the company that has had the greatest sales gain, resists new-product proliferation and is rarely first in any new market segment. Rather, it is superb at mobilizing its resources to obtain a position in a category once that category has been established by others.

Leadership—In 1968 *Dun's Review* attributed Philip Morris's success to the marketing-mindedness of its president, George Weisman.[2] But in 1965 *Financial World* noted Lorillard's intention to emphasize marketing by its appointment of Manuel Yellen as chairman and chief executive officer.[3] Mr. Yellen at that time had held almost every important executive post in the company's marketing organization. Despite the similar orientations of their leaders, the two companies have had very different results in the marketplace.

Fortuitous Events—In 1957 *Reader's Digest* published the results of a study on tar and nicotine. The study named Kent as the cigarette brand lowest in both substances and started a boom in sales for P. Lorillard that took its earnings from 67¢ a share in 1956 to $4.01 in 1958. Yet despite Lorillard's very enviable position of being in the market with the right product at the right time, its market share, which was approximately 12 percent in 1958, has gradually moved downward ever since, to less than 8 percent in 1976.

These are merely examples and certainly do not offer any conclusive proof that any or all of these factors are not crucial to success in any given situation. It is our thesis, however, that any one of these factors is insufficient to assure sustained success unless the management of the entire firm is organized and effectively mobilized to achieve that success.

By "organized and mobilized" we mean that managers must have a clear picture of what the company and their own units are attempting to accomplish; that units must be structured in such a way as to allow sufficient emphasis to be given to key businesses; that the relationships between units must allow for the maximum exploitation of synergistic potential; that the performance-planning and decision-making processes must be timely and effective; and that people must be qualified for their jobs, developed for bigger jobs, and motivated to direct their efforts toward the organization's objectives. These are major elements contributing to productive management climate.

The Nature of Climate

What is climate? There are probably as many answers to that question as there are writers on the subject, but we define "management climate" as managers' perceptions of the many characteristics of their organizations (such as those we have listed above) that have a direct impact upon their behavior. Viewed this way, the process of climate analysis becomes one of determining how managers at various levels and parts of an organization perceive the influences upon them, for these perceptions will cause them to take or fail to take specific actions.

Financial results, such as profitability, volume, and cost, have limitations as management tools because they tell what has happened, but not why. In contrast, climate analysis measures people's perceptions of how the organization is operating, and by doing so tells higher management how well its intentions are being understood and implemented.

Climate analysis speaks to the four aspects of an organization that management can change directly: strategy, structure, processes, and people. The technique deals with content issues, such as whether a company follows a strategy of being a pathfinder or a follower in an industry, as well as procedural issues, such as the extent to which a formal planning process exists. By uncovering and organizing managers' perceptions of these issues within the framework of actions open to top management, climate analysis provides a tool not only for gauging the health of an organization, but for improving the effectiveness of its managerial resources.

As a description of the organizational situation, climate analysis is not evaluative, nor is it a direct measure of the extent to which individual needs are satisfied. Rather, it is a diagnostic tool which allows top management to make evaluations knowledgeably and then focus on the needed changes. Furthermore, survey techniques such as those described in chapter 4 currently exist to translate the concept of climate analysis into an operational reality.

Climate and Success

In asking about an organization's climate, we are really asking how effectively that organization is mobilizing its human resources. Climate is the focus of a complex of forces within an organization upon its people. A knowledge of climate enables management to harness those forces toward the accomplishment of organizational goals. When this happens, a tremendous reservoir of energy and motivation becomes available.

Our research shows that climate as perceived by management is definitely related to a company's success. Taking a five-year average rate of growth in net profit as an indicator of sustained success, we found the more successful companies characterized by a formal system for planning that provides managers with a clear picture of where the company is going and how it intends to get there. This is backed up by a good deal of communication of relevant information—that is, information needed in decision-making and performance measurement. Finally, compensation is the glue that bonds individual contributions to company objectives. In short, people understand what is to be accomplished and how it is to be accomplished, how goals and activities are interrelated, what the measures of success are to be, and how they will share in the success that is attained.

Therefore, if better performance is desired, climate is the quality that must be changed before significant improvements in organizational functioning and individual behavior can be realized. Two case studies illustrate how a company can go about changing its climate to conform more closely to the success mode. One company is International Harvester, whose situation is discussed in detail in Robert Rock's *The Chief Executive Officer*; the other, a $250 million freestanding division of a major U.S. conglomerate, here called Ajax Products.[4]

In 1971 Brooks McCormick took over as chief executive officer (CEO) of International Harvester. Around that time, one financial analyst remarked, "In a classic sense—comparing profitability versus the long-term cost of capital—the company is in a process of liquidation."[5] International Harvester was making a margin of only 1.5 percent on sales and 3.9 percent on equity, even though a four-year surge in sales had placed the company at the $3 billion mark.

One of McCormick's early actions was to make, as he phrased it, "an agonizing appraisal of the management climate." In the course of conducting this climate survey, he concluded that the company harbored a number of myths about itself. The most damaging of these appeared to be

1. That the fundamental purpose of the company was implicitly understood, so that there was no need to detail it explicitly.
2. That by projecting steadily improving sales and earnings, management had established adequate goals, even though these had not been quantified, rationalized, or fixed in a definite time frame.
3. That the technology of communications allowed for the continuation of the company's traditional authoritarian management from the top.

As a result of these myths, some very fundamental climate weaknesses existed, including a lack of a sense of direction, insufficient delegation of authority and assignment of accountability, little flow of communication outside the established channels of command, a very short-range perspective on decision-making, and a general focus on activities rather than on results.

Armed with knowledge about his company's performance, which he believed stemmed clearly from the deficiencies in the management climate, McCormick took a three-pronged approach to improving managerial productivity. The first aspect was the establishment of a corporate planning process and the preparation of a strategic plan. Although development of the planning process was begun in May 1972, it is interesting to note that it took three years, until the summer of 1975, to produce a total corporate strategic plan. The plan's development involved the participation of approximately 3,000 managers across the company and depended upon the creation and implementation of new information systems before the company could have an accurate picture of how each of its components contributed to or detracted from the corporate objectives. Once completed, however, the plan laid the basis for a continued and detailed managerial blueprinting for a three-year period.

The second prong of the attack was the development of an accountability management system. New job descriptions spelling out specific responsibilities were developed for all management positions. These helped reveal unnecessary overlaps in accountabilities, as well as absences of or inadequate support for critical accountabilities. All key managers were then assessed in terms of their ability to discharge their responsibilities—whether they had the depth of managerial know-how, the problem-solving ability, and the desire to accept accountability required for their jobs. As a result of the assessments, conducted by the top officers of the corporation, individual and organizational deficiencies were pointed out. This review led to action designed to upgrade current individuals' capabilities and to recruit appropriate individuals when no suitable talents existed within the organization.

Finally, Harvester implemented a reward system, assuring that all executives were paid equitably and competitively with other companies. Furthermore, it installed an executive incentive program designed to offer management employees who held positions of major responsibility the opportunity to receive immediate rewards, reflecting their contributions to the company's success. This incentive program involved before-the-fact commitments about corporate, division, and individual performance and after-the-fact measurements against these commitments. Two additional incentive programs, a stock option, and a sustained performance award were established to assure that the company would maintain its continuity of performance and not sacrifice long-term objectives for short-term accomplishments.

In 1975 Harvester again conducted a climate study to determine what changes had been perceived by its management group. Very major gains were made. While the company was still at or below industry norms on many of the factors, it was obviously headed in the right direction. Its financial results for 1976 point to the same type of progress. On approximately $5.5 billion in sales, it obtained a net of 3.1 percent on sales and 11 percent on equity. Again, while these figures are not where the company would like to see them, they represent very substantial improvements on the company's position in 1971. The changes in climate, including changes in managerial processes, organizational structures, and people themselves, assure that the company will continue to obtain the improvement it seeks.

Our second example, Ajax Products, also represents an organization that was in deep trouble at the time that an initial climate survey was conducted. However, its smaller size allowed for more rapid change, and the very aggressive personality of the chief executive officer assured that the change would occur. In 1974 the company was faced with bulging inventories, slipping sales, an extremely tight cash position (which had caused some of its vendors to discontinue shipments), and a parent company that had lost its faith in the ability of this division to perform and was committed to selling it, in whole or in parts.

One of the first steps of a new chief executive officer, appointed in August 1974, was to conduct a climate analysis. A detailed look at the organization at that time indicated that the structure was inefficient insofar as certain key units did not have the appropriate impact, and therefore certain results were not being obtained. The company also suffered from inadequate controls and a definite lack of an information system that would allow for the establishment of workable controls.

In a speech, the new CEO highlighted his frustrations with these inadequate controls and his attempts to correct them: "I issued an edict in September that inventories were to go down . . . and they went up. In October, I pounded the table harder . . . and they went up even further. As a consequence, late in October I ordered that no components or supplies were to be received anywhere in the corporation during the month of November. This finally broke the back of the inventory buildup, although not without some attendant difficulties in terms of shortages of parts and additional unhappiness on the part of our vendors, and I suspect unhappiness on the part of some of our people who, I am certain, wondered if I knew what I was doing." This was certainly an extraordinary move to bring into line a situation that should be handled through normal managerial procedures.

The complete solution to the company's problems in this case took many more traditional directions, but again involved the basic areas of strategy, structure, processes, and people. Starting with sixteen members of key management, the president held biweekly meetings to inform them of the company's total condition and to involve them in the interrelated actions that would have to take place to effect rapid turnaround. In close working relationships, it was determined that not all individuals in the top management team were capable of handling their jobs in light of the increased demands for performance. Within a year, jobs had been reorganized to focus accountability, job descriptions were prepared, and the top management team was reduced to ten individuals.

The management information system capable of providing a basis for control was begun immediately, with final implementation projected for 1978. A number of functions, such as materials, credit, and data processing, were centralized at the corporate level, and all top staff and operating heads were brought together under one roof to shorten the lines of communication and increase integration. A new salary administration program was developed with the realization that the company would function with fewer but more capable and highly motivated individuals.

The climate survey was repeated in 1977, and it was found that significant gains had been made in almost all areas. Particularly strong improvements were perceived in the clarity of goals and the existence of plans to achieve those goals, the quality of communications, the orientation toward performance, and the quality of compensation. The financial performance of the company also showed dramatic improvement, with a 300 percent gain in income between 1974 and 1976.

These two examples serve to illustrate the basic point: that managerial productivity is a top-management responsibility and can have much more dramatic impact on company success than improvement in production-line performance. If a company is to achieve breakthroughs, it will do so as a result of strategic decisions related to research and development posture, expansion of capacity, marketing initiatives, and so forth. But significant achievements do not come about by happenstance. Rather, they occur because top management has created the appropriate climate in which to accomplish them.

These examples further support the thesis we tried to illustrate with our overview of the tobacco industry, that corporate success is not a function of one element of management. Instead, success is dependent upon a climate that mobilizes the management resources toward its attainment. Creating such a climate can require very pervasive changes in the organization and a great deal of time to accomplish.

Attitude Surveys versus Climate Analysis

The question is often raised whether "climate analysis" is merely a different name for "attitude survey." The two share a common mode of data collection—people are asked to report their reactions to their organizations in answer to a series of questions—but from that point on some very significant differences distinguish them.

First, the sample for an attitude survey normally starts at the bottom of the organization and works up, usually one or two levels, sometimes a little higher. But a climate survey starts at the top of the organization, usually with the president, chairman, or other leader, and works its way down, perhaps four or five levels. It typically includes between 150 and 300 people, as opposed to the thousands covered by an attitude survey in a large company.

Because each type of survey addresses itself to a very different group, the nature of the questions tends to be different. For example, a climate survey asks about the clarity of corporate goals, a topic inappropriate for the production-floor level. Therefore, because the two groups typically surveyed are dissimilar, the issues being investigated are distinct.

Second, attitude surveys grew out of a reaction to "scientific management," which viewed human beings as little more than units of production, and out of a fascination with the findings of the original Hawthorne studies and some of the early laboratory studies on leadership.[6] The thrust of this movement was to encourage worker satisfaction, which in turn would lead to greater production. Thus, many attitude surveys deal with employee satisfaction and focus upon supervisor-subordinate and work-group interactions, which are most influential on satisfaction.

Climate analysis has not evolved from this direction, but from a concept of enterprise management and a focus upon organizational performance. For an organization to be justified it must have a mission, and to accomplish that mission it must have a strategy, whether articulated or not, and people organized in some kind of structural relationship. The elements are related by a series of processes such as planning, decision-making, performance measurement, and so forth. As indicated above, the perception of these elements—strategy, structure, process, and people—that causes people to act in certain ways, is what we term climate. From this point of view, climate analysis is far from the measurement of satisfaction. It is truly the measure of the state of managerial health of the organization from the perspective of those who should know best—the managers themselves.

This book deals only with management climate, and gives no attention to attitude surveys. In it, the terms "climate" and "management climate" are used interchangeably.

Complexity of Climate

While the cases of International Harvester and Ajax Products exemplify the importance of climate in organizational success, they only hint at the complex nature of the relationship. Appendix A addresses the difficulties of assuming direct cause-effect relationships. A thorough understanding of climate involves knowledge of its sources, its measurement, its interpretation, and its meanings. The information presented in following chapters was developed from the systematic study of several hundred organizations to provide a foundation for applications of climate data to specific organizational situations.

Notes

1. Edmund Faltermayer, "Smokes by the Billion," *Fortune,* October 1976, p. 138.

2. "The Marketing Merlins of Philip Morris," *Dun's Review,* April 1968, pp. 32-33.

3. "Lorillard—Two-Way Appeal," *Financial World,* December 15, 1965, p. 13.

4. Robert H. Rock, *The Chief Executive Officer* (Lexington, Mass.: Lexington Books, D.C. Heath and Co., 1977), pp. 95-104.

5. Rock, p. 96.

6. F.J. Rothlesberger and W.J. Dixon, *Management and the Worker* (Cambridge, Mass.: Harvard University Press, 1939).

2 Antecedents of Climate

Climate does not come about spontaneously. It is not merely the result of luck or accident. Instead, it is caused by an aggregate of internal and external circumstances, some of which are more significant than others, some of which are fixed and some variable. Like a climate itself, the antecedents of climate can be delineated precisely and objectively. Those that are variable—usually internal circumstances—are most important, because they can potentially be controlled to bring about changes in future climate.

Of the many influences that contribute to the shaping of management climate, several relate to the previous history of the company—when it was founded, who the past leaders were, what they did to set certain patterns. The nature of the company itself—the type of business it is in, its market environment, its stage of development, whether it is capital intensive or labor intensive—is also a factor. Other external influences involve technology, governmental relationships, and social structure.

Although these circumstances all come into play in setting climate, by far the most important factor is the current leadership of the company, that individual or group of individuals who has the greatest say in the directions the company takes. The values displayed through the actions of top management— the policy statements they issue, the organizational structure they create, the reward systems they introduce, the people they hire, and the people they promote—most strongly determine the climate.

External Forces

External influences can be broken down into a number of basic environments: social, technological, market, economic, and governmental.

The social environment reflects the culture in which the company exists, specifically such matters as its definition of success and the organizational models provided by family, religion, and education. Attitudes toward such questions as obedience versus independence, tradition versus innovation, achievement versus power or affiliation are essential to the social environment. For example, although they produce the same product and use similar technologies, American and Japanese automobile manufacturers would have dissimilar climates because of inherent national differences concerning matters such as authority, security, and personal expectations.

11

Perhaps the most immediate expression of personal expectations as a social force affecting climate can be perceived in employee demands. While many demands arise from particular situations within a company, the general context is usually determined by conditions in the society as a whole. For example, in the past, when the majority of the work force endured dismal twelve-hour days, the issues involved safety and security: being cold and wet, facing danger and fatigue, fearing arbitrary firing. But today, with the dramatic improvement in the basic work setting, demands involve issues at a very different level, such as having work that allows people to utilize and develop their talents. Therefore, managers today cannot assume that a climate in which security and personal well-being are high will automatically satisfy individual needs and result in committed employees.

The nature of the work force itself is a strong determinant of personal expectations and thus of climate. In recent years, we have seen a movement away from relatively uneducated workers, grateful just to have a job, toward educated, almost affluent employees. This new group is more independent and unwilling to accept authoritarian practices; these individuals expect to have a say in whatever affects their lives. Therefore, management must recognize and accommodate its practices to these attitudes in order to maximize performance.

It is difficult to delineate all the influences of the technological environment on climate, but some generalizations can be made. For instance, in a company where capital expenditures for equipment are great and relatively little skill is required from the labor force, the contribution of employees will be valued much less than in a company where the efforts of skilled people provide the product. A business in a field of rapidly changing technology will require different adjustments from employees and therefore a different management style from one in a field where the technology is constant.

The market environment results in different climates. An industry that is highly competitive and dynamic requires adaptability and innovation; to survive, an organization must have a style that encourages risk-taking and individual autonomy. However, these same characteristics could be counterproductive in a mature industry in which the greatest challenge is to improve efficiency in producing a well-defined, stable product line. Here, a more structured, controlling style of management is called for.

A strong or weak economy has a climate impact. If money is tight, control over expenditures becomes tighter and restriction of initiative could possibly result. In general, a tighter economy makes people more apprehensive and cautious, while an expanding economy makes them more flexible and open to change and development.

Government influences climate indirectly through its controls on the economy, such as fiscal and monetary policies and tax and international trade tariffs, and directly through the imposition of regulations. For example, as the government enacts new legislative requirements, companies often must create new jobs to comply. Regulations, such as those related to pollution control or equal employment opportunity, place restrictions on companies. These in turn may be translated into restrictions on people within the company and may even cause a change in management style, with more centralized control over certain operations.

All of these external environments are conditions that a company cannot ignore. It cannot change the market in which it competes, or trends in the economy, or the forces that shape the entire society. Yet although they are givens, these environments usually have different meanings for different organizations in different situations. Therefore, top management must acknowledge them and adapt its planning to account for them. How management reacts to external factors can be more important than the factors themselves in shaping climate.

Organizational History

As an antecedent of climate, the history of an organization may be regarded as both external and internal, external because it is a fixed legacy which may be consciously or unconsciously imposed on current top management, and internal because it may be a major determinant of current management style, manifested in the decisions made each day.

The traditions of a company seem to have a lingering power in establishing policies and procedures. They become "the way we do things in our business," and these values are passed on from one generation of managers to the next. In fact, some evidence suggests that managers are chosen more for their values than for their abilities.[1] The company's image may influence the types of individuals who apply, those who are hired, and, ultimately, the kind of interpersonal environment that is established.

Often, outsiders with different values are brought in to manage a firm only when the situation is obviously bad enough to require fundamental change. For example, the traditions and lore of the railroads rendered their management incapable of thinking about the transportation business as a whole. Some businesses that survived the Depression were unable to adapt to policies of high financial leverage or aggressive advertising and therefore missed the opportunities of the postwar growth period. When existing attitudes are no longer capable of dealing with present business conditions, outsiders are sought. What usually results is a rethinking of former values and traditions, and this process has a very profound impact upon climate. These changes in themselves may mark the beginning of a new phase in the organization's history.

The Role of Management

As top management examines the company's position—the business environment, its type of business, the nature of the competition, its own resources—it develops certain objectives and orients the company toward achieving them. Part of this orientation process is the development and modification of structures and systems for managing the enterprise that help define what is expected from people and what they can expect in return from the company.

The way that top management wants these structures and systems to work—the behavior they wish to encourage—can be considered the *intended climate.* For example, developing appropriate performance objectives for each organizational unit and providing regular and frequent evaluation of performance against those objectives creates a climate with a central focus on performance. Therefore, the leadership style of top management stimulates particular patterns of motivation and creates expectations for certain kinds of behavior.

A number of well-constructed psychological experiments have been conducted to measure the effects of different management styles. One of the major findings has been that distinct organizational climates can be created by varying the style of the leader. These climates can in turn significantly affect both job performance and the satisfaction that people get from their work environment.

In one of these experiments, individuals were put into three simulated companies in which all aspects of the work were the same.[2] Each company contained fifteen employees matched with respect to age, sex, background, psychological need pattern, and other personality characteristics. Each company duplicated the others in its structure; the technology and essential tasks were the same; the physical locations were identical. The companies were organized functionally into production, product development, and control or accounting departments. Only the company leaders, the presidents, differed.

The first president focused on structure and created a very formal hierarchy in which individual roles and authorities were tightly defined. Communication took place only through formal channels, and deviations from the rules were not tolerated. The outcome of this style was highly unsatisfactory. The performance (profitability) results and innovation were low. In addition, general satisfaction was low, and feelings of personal responsibility declined.

The second organization was characterized by a loose, informal structure which focused upon people and teamwork. Conflict was avoided through managerial attention to the development and well-being of the workers. A high degree of general satisfaction resulted, but innovation was only moderate and the company actually ran a net loss. Although people's feelings toward each other were very positive, and there was a great deal of mutual interdependence, personal responsibility declined.

The president of the third organization stressed achievement and motivation through personal goal-setting and individual responsibility. High productivity was praised by him, and management supported efforts to be creative. Excellent performance was rewarded both psychologically and monetarily, and frequent competitive data was provided as the target to beat. Although no formal channels were set up, people were encouraged to communicate with others if they needed help to get the job done. The results of this group were considerably better than those of the other two. Profitability, innovation, and satisfaction were all high. Attitudes toward others were open and cordial, and personal feelings of competence and responsibility increased.

The results of this experiment demonstrate that individuals in each of these three organizations experienced very different climates because of the behavior of their leaders. In part, this behavior consisted of the way in which the leader structured the task. Specifically, in the first organization, the task was made very formal and standardized. For all intents and purposes, the best way had been found and institutionalized; there could be no deviation. In the second, personal satisfaction became the primary goal and little attention was paid to the organization's mission. In the third organization, only the results counted. Individuals were free to experiment and take personal responsibility for discovering new and better ways of doing things. In addition, the president himself ensured that individuals would receive feedback about how well they were doing on their task.

Because these three companies were small organizations created for the purpose of the study, objections could be raised over their artificiality and their size. However, research among large and complex organizations verifies the dominant force of leadership in establishing climate.[3] In fact, this research clearly indicates that the influence of the management is so strong that even climates of companies in the same industry within the same country can differ radically from one another. On the other hand, different divisions or departments within a company tend to have very similar management climates—a definite indication that a pervading influence exists in the company, and a strong suggestion that the influence of top management reaches deep into the organization. This influence can be seen in the answers to such questions as

> To what extent are people free to take the independent actions necessary to carry out their job responsibilities?

> How much are people encouraged to take reasonable risks to increase the effectiveness of the organization?

> How much support do employees receive from higher levels of management?

The answers to such questions are as much perceptions as they are objective facts. Remember that the behavioral goals of the systems and procedures established by the leaders are only the intended climate. How a manager or president behaves is not as significant as how subordinates perceive that behavior. These perceptions are their signals as to how they should perform their own functions and thus define the climate of the company. Therefore, communication down through the management channels is vital.

Notes

1. Ronald J. Grey and George G. Gordon, "Risk-Taking Managers: Who Gets the Top Jobs?" *Management Review*, November 1978, p. 11.

2. George H. Litwin, "Climate and Motivation: An Experimental Study," in *Organizational Climate: Exploration of a Concept*, eds. Renato Tagiuri and George H. Litwin (Cambridge, Mass.: Harvard University Press, 1968), pp. 169-90.

3. George G. Gordon and Bonnie E. Goldberg, "Is There a Climate for Success?" *Management Review*, May 1977, pp. 37-44.

3 Communication and Motivation

Climate consists of perceptions of the written, oral, and behavioral messages sent from higher levels of management. These perceptions, however, do not always coincide with the messages themselves. Other sources of perception may modify or even undermine official communications, because of two possible causes: employees may misperceive the intended nature of the messages, or management itself may not be aware of the unintended, subtle messages that it is sending.

While reality provides an important anchor point, perceptions of reality (which do not always coincide with it) are more directly responsible for controlling individual actions. Consider the captain who runs his boat aground: his actions are guided not by the reality that the channel is too shallow, but by his perception that it is safe. In the same way, top management, for reasons of long-term development, may desire a profit center manager to try innovative yet costly approaches to increasing the company's market share. However, if that manager believes instead, rightly or wrongly, that his career depends more on maintaining current profits, he may be quite hesitant to innovate.

Two basic approaches to climate measurement exist. The first is to analyze the factual situation through such characteristics as the number of levels of management, the span of control, and the salary levels. The second is to analyze perceptions. Most work in the field employs the second approach, on the assumption that asking the people involved is the only effective method of investigating the climate being experienced.

The summation of individuals' perceptions of the various management issues forms the basis of climate. The fact that these views will not always coincide with reality is an integral part of climate analysis, not a shortcoming of the survey instrument. For instance, if compensation is perceived as being low competitively when it is actually above average, the problem does not necessarily lie in the instrument used to measure perceptions of compensation, but is most likely in the communication of compensation policy and its competitive position throughout the organization.

Communication of Intended Climate

The intended climate is communicated formally through means such as organizational structure, policy statements, and project designs, and informally through the conclusions drawn from specific management behavior—what units get most

17

top management attention, which individuals progress most rapidly, what happens when targets are not met, and so forth. These messages are transmitted to the levels of management that interact with top management, and these managers in turn communicate a climate to their own units in both formal and informal ways. As the intended climate is translated through successive layers of the organization, it encounters certain barriers which can change the nature of the communication. These changes are usually responsible for the failure of an intended climate to materialize.

The first barrier is the tendency of the individual to perceive selectively, taking in those messages he wishes to receive and screening out those he does not. A fundamental influence on the ability to perceive a message accurately is the individual's personal needs and motivations. While the head of a company may be motivated in one manner, those under him may have different needs. These differences can cause misinterpretations of intentions.

A second barrier also relates to motivation. In this case, the individual perceives the intentions correctly but because of his personality modifies the intended climate to fit his own managerial style, a situation discussed below under "Motivations and Perceptions."

A third barrier, different in nature from the first two, results when informal messages contradict the formal ones. Top management's actual behavior may not support the formal systems designed to produce the intended climate. For example, when top management delegates broad approval authority and sets up reporting procedures on a results-only basis, it is encouraging a decentralized management style where lower levels of management enjoy a high degree of freedom. However, if actual experience with this system indicates that people are severely penalized when a mistake is made, subordinate managers will seek approval from superiors before exercising authority.

Thus, while climate is set initially by top management, a variety of factors can cause significant modification as it travels down through the different layers of the organization and across its different units. Climate analysis through measurement of perceptions can determine whether the directions that top management wishes to establish are being translated into actions.

Motivations and Perceptions

As noted above, individual motivations are often a filter through which messages are distorted. Motivation can be described as a drive to satisfy an internal need. Because all behavior is motivated by some unfulfilled internal need, it is not accurate to speak of "motivating someone." Leadership does not create motivations; rather, it taps those that an individual already possesses, by providing the opportunity to work toward fulfilling them.

Acknowledgement of this fundamental psychological premise has essential implications for managers attempting to create a specific climate. First of all, a climate cannot be imposed unilaterally because it is very difficult to make people behave in ways that clash with their personalities. Since people tend to interpret messages in a manner that accommodates them to personal needs, they will, if necessary, selectively perceive information about intended climate so that they can pursue behavior patterns with which they are comfortable.

For instance, suppose the president of a company wishes the heads of its two operating divisions to emphasize the goals of increased profitability and increased market share. One division head, motivated by a strong need for achievement and little concern for personal security, may focus on the marketing objective, with only a sketchy plan of how the money spent on this goal will be recovered through larger production runs. Because of personal motivations, this head places more emphasis on the riskier marketing objective as the basis for operating strategy.

The second division head is a conservative individual motivated more by the need to maintain the status quo than to reach out in new directions. Knowing that market penetration is a very expensive process, this manager may opt to cut costs in order to increase profitability to such a desirable level that the money will then be available for additional marketing activity. Thus, the same overall objectives can be translated into totally different tactical approaches.

Of course, the fact that individuals have different motivations does not mean that managers are helpless in implementing new procedures and modifying climate. First, clear and reinforced communications are the most direct method for avoiding misperceptions. Further, over a period of time, an organization tends to hire and promote people with attributes suited to its management style.[1] Also, most organizations take into account the strengths and weaknesses of its key people in structuring its activities. Thus, either the organization can change to fit the people, or the mix of people can change to fit the organization.

Upward Communication

So far, the discussion of perception and climate has emphasized barriers to the transmission of messages from top management downward through the company. However, the converse problem can also exist. Messages coming upward may be restricted or misperceived.

Restriction occurs because of the power relationships involved. Subordinates may pass on only the information that they think their superiors want to receive—that is, information that reinforces the validity of the decisions made by those superiors or their methods of operation. Various reasons could explain the actions of these subordinates. They may want to cover up for their own real or imagined failings; they may want to enhance their own positions by being remembered as the conveyers of good news; or they may want to avoid the reactions of disappointed leaders. Whatever the reason, top management does not receive a totally accurate picture of the climate within the organization.

Because leaders themselves are not immune from human needs, even if they get accurate information from below they may misperceive it in ways that are in keeping with their original intentions or expectations of success. A combination of restricting subordinates and misperceiving superiors can lead to severe distortions of messages.

These barriers to upward communication can be as detrimental to climate as inaccurate downward communication. If those responsible for establishing climate do not understand the real situation in their organizations, they will fail to correct deficiencies and instead make additional decisions that may compound problems. Here again climate analysis provides a means of avoiding such difficulties, because it results in what is in effect an upward report of conditions throughout the organization, a report based on objective measurement rather than on hearsay or assumptions—that is, a report presented in a manner that minimizes misperception.

Actual Versus Perceived Pay Practices

The area of pay practices provides a dramatic example of the potential conflict between perceptions and actuality. All too often employees have a negative view of their company's compensation system, even though objective data indicate that it is a high-paying firm.

A company committed to offering highly competitive compensation expects a return on this investment in improved employee performance. If, however, employees fail to recognize this benefit, the potential motivational impact of the pay plan is lost. If they believe pay scales are poor, the impact may even be demoralizing.

Such misperception is not an isolated problem, but may be the rule rather than the exception. Comparative data on a variety of companies reveal very little correspondence between a company's pay position in the marketplace and overall management perceptions of its pay practices.[2] Virtually no statistical relationship existed between total management measures of actual and perceived pay practices. In other words, management-level employees of companies that were actually high-paying did not consider the compensation offered by their companies to be satisfactory. This result contrasts with the close relationship between managers' belief in high external competitiveness and their satisfaction with pay.

While perceptions of pay may not accurately reflect a company's competitive position, they nevertheless govern people's feelings of pay satisfaction. Therefore, to achieve maximum effectiveness, a well-paying organization must accurately communicate its competitive stance through the management ranks.

We see that the subject of climate is inextricably tied to that of communications. The climate one perceives is established through a myriad of messages. Some of these are well defined and reality-based. Others are really the results of a lack of communication, and where this occurs, imagination, preconceptions, and personal motivation take over to formulate the climate. To the degree that top management wishes to establish a particular climate pattern, it must communicate that pattern frequently and extensively, and must furthermore establish a clear channel of communication upward from below to assure that the message sent was the one received.

Notes

1. Ronald J. Grey and George G. Gordon, "Risk-Taking Managers: Who Gets the Top Jobs?" *Management Review,* November 1978, pp. 8-13.
2. "Hay Compensation Comparison" and "Hay Management Climate Survey," annual surveys conducted by Hay Associates, Philadelphia.

**Part II
Evaluating Climate**

4 Climate Measurement

To comprehend climate, one must be aware of what attributes are measured and why those specific attributes and measurement techniques are chosen. Because climate, although a tangible condition of an organization's operation, does not have an objective identity until analyzed, the nature of the survey instrument itself helps to create that identity. That is, the assumptions the survey makes concerning the origins of climate, the audience with which it deals, and the information it seeks will all lead to a specific type of result. Therefore, before the measurement instrument is prepared, its developers must have an understanding of what climate is and what it is not. Our own answers to these questions have brought about the approach discussed in this book.

Two Perspectives of Climate

Two views of the nature of organizational climate are possible. The broader view is based on the premise that climate is the total set of organizational attributes that influence job-relevant behavior in current and potential employees. This inclusive definition conceives of these influences as qualities that may be grouped into specific categories, such as organizational strategy, structure, processes, and people.

Most management planning deals with aspects of this concept of climate, implicitly or explicitly. Such questions as the competitive position of a company, its entry into new markets, and its relationship to the public at large call for an examination of the company's strategies, its resources, the structure for focusing momentum in a certain area, and similar aspects. Thus, stimulated by this concept, every company engages in some type of climate measurement in its normal planning process.

However, missing in this definition is a consideration of individual motivations, the element inherent in the second view of climate. Motivation is a screen through which an individual modifies his view of reality, and because a person behaves in accordance with that view or perception, motivation often results in a modification of the characteristic itself, as illustrated in figure 4-1. For instance, if a manager *perceives* that a performance appraisal system is intended to "weed out the deadwood," he will operate the process in that manner, even though its intended objective is to direct and increase everyone's performance. Thus, the perception becomes the reality.

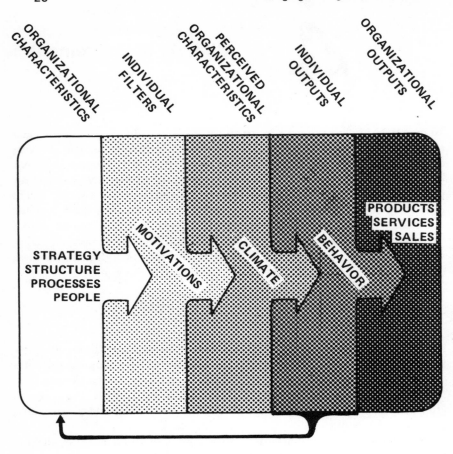

ORGANIZATIONAL CHARACTERISTICS

INDIVIDUAL FILTERS

PERCEIVED ORGANIZATIONAL CHARACTERISTICS

INDIVIDUAL OUTPUTS

ORGANIZATIONAL OUTPUTS

STRATEGY
STRUCTURE
PROCESSES
PEOPLE

MOTIVATIONS

CLIMATE

BEHAVIOR

PRODUCTS
SERVICES
SALES

Figure 4-1. A Model of Organizational Functioning

In this second view, organizational climate consists of the qualities of the company as perceived by its present and potential employees. (The importance of such perceptions has been discussed at length in chapter 3). As the model in figure 4-1 suggests, organizational characteristics may be measured in one of two ways: the characteristics themselves can be measured, or the perceptions of those characteristics can be used. These perspectives parallel the two views of climate, but, as we also suggest in the model, *the climate—that which most directly influences behavior—is the perception of reality, not the reality itself.* Furthermore, neither the characteristics themselves nor the climate can change without potentially causing change in the order.

To the degree that the model is valid, quite different conclusions can be drawn from measurement at the two points. For instance, we can cite cases where a formal planning system yielding written plans exists, whereas perceptions indicate the absence of plans to accomplish objectives. In these cases, the plans are paper exercises which then get filed away until the next year and have no real influence on managerial activities. Which fact is more pertinent to managing the organization, that a planning process produces plans or that managers do not perceive the existence of plans to direct their everyday activities? We have clearly opted for the latter, constructing a methodology to measure perceptions of organizational characteristics rather than one to measure the characteristics themselves.

An Approach to Measuring Climate

Attempts to measure organizational climate through the perceptual approach have resulted in the generation of a number of structures which are more similar than different. A review of several such studies found four dimensions common to them: individual autonomy; degree of structure imposed on the position; reward orientation; and consideration, warmth, and support.[1]

Thus, when Hay Associates began a program of research and development in climate analysis in 1969, a good deal of guidance was available. Yet we pursued some different paths (for instance, a consideration, warmth, and support dimension has never emerged in our own work) because of some basic differences in the way we viewed the role of management climate. Our experience strongly suggested that regardless of size, industry, or age of a company, top management was the most important influence upon the way in which the company was run. Therefore, the goal of each study was to measure the results, intended or unintended, of this influence.

Our early approaches to climate measurement blended a recognition of the published literature with the problems and requirements of the particular organization being studied. Each study began with a series of interviews and examination of organization charts, policy memos, and so forth. Within each company, those interviewed typically included all vice presidents and higher executives and a small sample of individuals at other management levels. The focus was on management climate as a pervasive element of the company rather than as a manifestation of small-group, superior-subordinate relationships.

Following the interview process, a questionnaire was developed to elaborate systematically and quantifiably on the initial information obtained. Dimensions considered important in the literature which had not emerged during the interviews were also included. This questionnaire was then completed anonymously, most usually by all individuals at the four organizational levels below the president. While the analysis differed from company to company, the statistical techniques of factor and cluster analysis were typically used in data reduction.

As the sample grew over the first few dozen companies surveyed, it became obvious that a good deal of the information being obtained from specific companies was equally relevant for most companies. Such topics as the quality of delegation or the clarity of organizational goals were important issues, regardless of the particular company under investigation.

Therefore, in 1974, after four years of individually tailored studies, a standard approach was developed in which the format was based upon items that had proved to be consistently useful in the previous studies. In addition, since experience had shown that the data provided greatest insights when interpreted against norms and since many companies were interested in tracking climate change, an annual Management Climate Survey was instituted. This afforded the opportunity to collect data on a number of companies at roughly the same time and to repeat that data collection yearly to allow companies to conduct before-and-after evaluations of new programs that they may have instituted.

The following discussion, as well as most of the data presented in this book, is based on the Hay Management Climate Survey. This is, however, not the only standardized survey of its type. A number of others exist, most notably that designed by the Survey Research Center of the University of Michigan.[2] Thus, the general characteristics of the Hay survey are not unique and may apply to other surveys as well.

The Hay Survey began in 1974 with twenty-nine participants and has grown each year since then. Including multiple participation, more than 250 studies have been conducted since the inception of the survey. Almost all the participating firms can be described as medium to large in size, and include manufacturing, utilities, mining, banking, insurance, professional services, publishing, and hospitals.

While the survey form has undergone some revision over the years, forty-eight of the fifty-seven items currently used in the standard survey instrument were used consistently. Factor analytical research was conducted to structure the item pool into a format designed for efficient presentation of results. Factor analysis is basically a process that seeks to determine the structure underlying a large, complex set of data. In this case, although we were dealing with more than fifty items, our previous experience had made it clear that there are fewer than fifty basic perspectives from which managers would view the organization. Thus, we examined the extent to which the answers to each question were similar to the answers to every other question. The factor analysis technique enabled us to identify groups of items that tended to have similar responses no matter what organization was being studied. For example, we found that if people believed that their company demanded high levels of performance from its employees, they also reported that managers were held personally accountable for what they produced or failed to produce. These and other items responded to in a similar fashion were characterized under the heading of "performance orientation." Eight such dimensions were obtained in a series of factor analyses. These eight dimensions, while related to one another, provide eight windows through which an organization can be examined and its management dynamics understood.

Eight Climate Dimensions

The items included in the standard climate survey (appendix B) are grouped into the following eight climate dimensions:

1. Organizational Clarity—the degree to which the goals and plans of the organization are clearly perceived by its members.
2. Decision-Making—the extent to which decisions are made in a rational manner, effectively implemented, and systematically evaluated in terms of their effects.
3. Organizational Integration—the extent to which various subunits cooperate and communicate effectively toward the achievement of overall organizational objectives.
4. Management Style—the extent to which people perceive encouragement to use their own initiative in performing their jobs, feel free to question constraints, and sense support when needed from higher levels of management.
5. Performance Orientation—the extent to which emphasis is placed upon individual accountability for clearly defined results and high levels of performance.
6. Organizational Vitality—the extent to which people see the organization as a dynamic one, as reflected by the venturesomeness of its goals, the innovativeness of its decisions, and its responsiveness to changing conditions.
7. Compensation—the extent to which the compensation system is seen as equitable, competitive, and related to performance.
8. Human Resource Development—the extent to which individuals perceive opportunities within the organization to develop to their full potential.

The specific items under each dimension are scattered throughout the questionnaire, and each is presented to elicit responses on a seven-point scale, with 1 normally being the least favorable rating and 7 the most favorable. The format for the questions in the performance orientation dimension is illustrated in figure 4-2.

Questionnaires are distributed to participants through the normal channels of written communication used by the organization. The participant receives a covering letter, usually signed by the head of the organization. This letter describes the purpose of the survey, assures individual anonymity, requests cooperation, and directs that the survey forms be returned by a specific date.

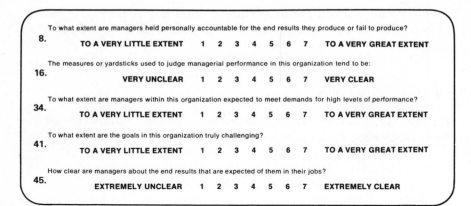

Figure 4-2. Questions in the Performance Orientation Dimension

The questionnaire is also accompanied by an envelope addressed to the agent conducting the survey, whether internal staff or external consultant. The use of an agent, rather than line management, to receive the survey forms further guarantees anonymity and fosters a high return rate. Our own experience indicates that the return rate is normally over 80 percent.

Once the responses from the organization under consideration are analyzed, the results are compared with those of more than 25,000 managers from the more than 100 companies surveyed previously. From these data a percentile score is computed for each item. This score represents the rank of the organization compared with all other organizations studied, with some adjustment for size. So, if a company scores at the sixty-third percentile on a particular item, then it scores higher than approximately 62 percent and lower than 37 percent of the companies studied.

The reported results show the organization's percentile scores for each of the items and the eight dimensions. Results can also show differences by management level, organizational unit, or a number of other demographics. Figure 4-3, representing data from a hypothetical company, shows the format in which we normally present the results by dimension. Figure 4-4 shows a format in which item scores are compared. While the graphs in these figures are for the total responses from the hypothetical company, reports may also include equivalent graphs for subgroups.

An example of the types of subgroup responses that a climate survey can isolate may be seen through a listing of the categories of audiences compiled in various studies we have conducted. While any particular study would rarely

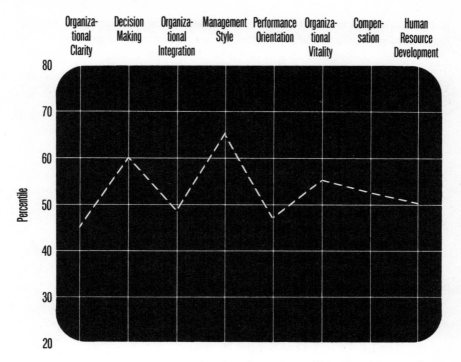

Figure 4-3. Graphic Presentation of Dimension Results

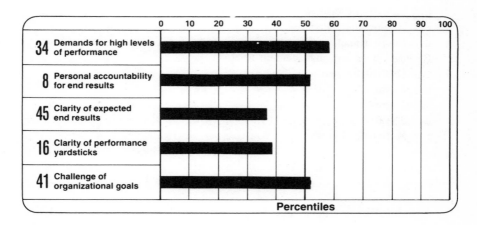

Figure 4-4. Graphic Presentation of Item Results

include more than three categories, the following listing provides a sense of the range of categories that might be applied to any particular investigation:

1. By functional area
    a. Marketing
    b. Manufacturing
    c. Research & Development
    d. Finance
    e. Information Services
    f. Personnel & Labor Relations
    g. Law
    h. Other
2. By years with the company
    a. Less than 3 years
    b. 3 to 10 years
    c. Over 10 years
3. By present management reporting level
    a. Level 1—President and CEO
    b. Level 2—Executive Vice Presidents
    c. Level 3—Vice Presidents
    d. Level 4—Directors and General Managers
    e. Level 5—People who report to Level 4
4. By division
    a. Consumer Products
    b. Industrial Products
    c. Maintenance Services
    d. International
5. By years at present management level
    a. Less than 1 year
    b. 1 year
    c. 2 years
    d. 3 years
    e. More than 3 years

Notes

1. John N.P. Campbell, Marvin D. Dunnette, Edward E. Lawler, III, and Karl E. Weick, Jr., *Managerial Behavior, Performance and Effectiveness* (New York: McGraw-Hill, 1970), p. 389-394.

2. James C. Taylor and David G. Bowers, *Survev of Organizations* (Ann Arbor: University of Michigan, 1972).

5 Understanding the Dimensions of Climate

Although no one climate is the ideal for all organizations (see chapter 8, "The 'Right' Climate"), some basic generalizations may be made concerning the significance of certain scores in each of the eight dimensions. However, even these generalizations must be reconsidered in light of the special circumstances of the organization being studied. The particular significance of climate information, especially suggestions for planning and future actions, can be obtained only through individualized analysis. The guidelines which follow provide a basis for such analysis.

Organizational Clarity

Organizational clarity exists when employees perceive the missions, objectives, processes, and activities of the enterprise as purposeful, rational, and fully communicated. People experience these characteristics as unifying influences which can enhance cooperation and collaboration.

A further influence on clarity is the extent to which planning and goal-setting processes provide clear purposes and a context for performance. These processes are important to the future success of the organization because they represent systematic efforts to control the future rather than remain reactive to it. When effective, these efforts provide a lucid perspective of the enterprise's mission. People know where the company is going and how it intends to get there. The framework they receive for relating their personal objectives to those of the enterprise allows them to experience feelings of belonging and identification.

Therefore, the key factor in creating a rational and challenging climate is not only the existence of goals, but also the effective communication of clear, complete, realistic goals and plans. This concept emphasizes the important role of explicit strategies, plus the awareness and acceptance of them by managers, as major factors in establishing the basis and nature of organizational climate.

In companies scoring high on this dimension, employees feel that the organization has clear goals and relatively complete and well-defined plans for meeting them. Moreover, not only do the goals provide a useful context for day-to-day operating, but both the planning and decision-making processes are accomplished with a view toward long-range outcomes of the enterprise. Therefore, the high-clarity company is one in which top management is oriented toward organizational performance planning and has conveyed that message downward. People understand what the organization intends to accomplish, how the objectives affect their own job goals, and what they must do to contribute effectively to organizational performance.

Employees in low-scoring companies or low-scoring units of high-scoring companies are probably unsure of the company's purposes. They may be unclear about their own jobs, the effectiveness of managerial planning, the future of the unit, or similar factors. The uncertainty about aims, objectives, and future purposes suggested by low scores on organizational clarity can result from either a lack of adequate goal orientation or a failure to communicate organizational objectives effectively. Frequently, low scores also reflect the effects of real change in the enterprise, such as a recent or anticipated merger, acquisition, or divestiture; major reorganization announced without participative planning and preparation; a real or feared change in management style; or a change in top management personnel.

In any case, low scores require careful consideration by management. The causes should be understood, if possible, and appropriate corrective action taken. Such action may be as simple as explicit communication of complete information, or it may require redesign of the planning process or, perhaps, group problem-solving actions to isolate and correct the causes of the low clarity.

Decision-Making

Decision-making is the process of choosing a course of action or selecting one from a group of alternatives. Climate survey results reflect perceptions of the extent to which decisions are based on appropriate informational input and are effectively implemented and systematically evaluated.

From one point of view, a manager's primary function and challenge is decision-making. This function encompasses both the decisions the manager makes and the manager's responsibility to assure the quality, timeliness, accuracy, and effectiveness of decisions made by subordinates. If it were possible to identify and collect all decisions made by all managers, one could assess the overall decision-making effectiveness of an enterprise.

The difficulty, if not impossibility, of collecting such information is not usually an issue, because results, such as growth, profit, and new products, provide indirect measures of the effectiveness of decision-making. Such measures, since they are related to business performance, suffice for most purposes. However, these general indicators are not very useful in assessing decision-making as a management process or as one of the variables that reflects the health and strength of an organization.

Perceptions of the decision-making process can be measured, since managers at all levels have a sense of what information is used in the process. They can also provide judgments of the extent to which decisions are effectively translated into action and the degree to which consequences of decisions are systematically evaluated. The climate survey reflects the expression of these perceptions.

High ratings on this factor indicate employee perceptions that the decision-making process is rational and effective, with relevant decisions being made at appropriate levels, effectively translated into action, and systematically monitored in terms of their effects. Basically, high ratings indicate confidence in the company's ability to make effective decisions, implement them, and then evaluate their impact.

Low ratings can stem from a number of sources. For one, the company may not be harnessing the information necessary to make wise decisions. Such perceptions result when information systems are poorly conceived or ineffectively used. Decision-makers may not recognize or accept the need for more information or more accurate, pertinent information, even when it is available. Further, decision-making may not be taking place at the appropriate management levels.

A second reason for low ratings might lie in an uncertain organizational structure which makes different parts of the organization feel accountable for the same areas or feel that the accountability for some important area is not clearly assigned. This lack of clarity in the structure will naturally lead to problems in the process of decision-making. Also, where structures are unclear, appropriate performance information often is not available for decision-making.

Low ratings also result when higher-level management is seen as failing to take actions necessary to implement and evaluate decisions. A communication problem may be responsible for such situations. That is, the prescribed actions for implementing decisions may not be communicated adequately to people at the appropriate level. Similarly, senior management may be systematically evaluating the consequences of decisions, but neglecting to communicate the results to appropriate parties. On the other hand, a failure to translate decisions into action plans may be the real problem. Greater insight into this situation can be provided by examining the results of the integration and organizational clarity dimensions.

Organizational Integration

Each unit of a complex organization exists to achieve results essential to the success of the enterprise. Therefore, management must plan the activities of the various units so that they integrate into an effective total effort. Overall results are usually accumulated for measurement into sales volume, products manufactured, customers served, or similar quantification. These company results provide a common base to which the various units can relate their specific results. However, the process of achieving results is dependent upon communication and cooperation through many formal and informal channels. These interactions take place as time and events dictate, in patterns so complex as to be rarely articulated. Organizational integration reflects the perceptions of these interactions.

High scores on this factor indicate that people believe units understand each other's objectives, needs, and problems. Units are seen as communicating freely in establishing modes for interunit functioning. High scores are likely when high levels of cooperation and collaboration exist. Such scores tend to accompany a participative management style if such a style is set by top management.

Proper evaluation of the results on this factor must consider the degree of interunit functioning required and encouraged by the organizational structure, the processes for allocating resources, and the nature of the business itself. For example, it is typical to find rather low integration in a professional organization, such as a law firm or an accounting firm, where people function more or less as individual contributors. Higher integration is typical in a manufacturer producing multiple products within a single product line. Organizations differ in the degree of integration required for effective overall performance. Judgments and decisions about the amount of integration required and the appropriateness and methods for change are tasks of top management.

Low scores indicate low interunit cooperation and lack of understanding between units of each other's goals or difficulties. People in an enterprise with moderately low scores may not require high integration to operate effectively. However, such ratings can also point to inadequate integration for the best interests of the enterprise. In such an organization, communications may be poor, interrelationships unclear, or people unwilling to expend effort in support of other units.

Ratings on integration must be viewed in the framework of the organization's missions, structure, and processes. However, this qualification should not automatically provide a rationalization for low ratings without very careful examination. Very low ratings in any type of organization are probably indicative of basic unresolved conflicts which adversely influence the organization's ability to function most effectively.

Management Style

Management must assure that organizational objectives are achieved. To accomplish this difficult task efficiently requires that a large part of the effort be passed along to those at lower levels. Management style is the complex of behaviors and procedures for accomplishing this delegation. One way to measure this style is to ask subordinates how they perceive the latitude afforded and the constraints imposed on them by higher levels of management. The management style dimension, therefore, indicates the extent and pattern of delegated authority in the organization as seen through the eyes of those to whom it is delegated. In this context, delegation is more than the process of informing a manager that he is responsible for a given result; it is the setting of limits within which he is able to affect that result.

In organizations scoring high on this dimension, managers have considerable freedom to determine and take the actions they deem necessary to perform their jobs best. They are encouraged to think innovatively, to take reasonable risks, and to speak up about problems or constraints. This condition is generally termed a delegative or participative style, in contrast to the centralized, more directive management style indicated by low ratings on this dimension.

Interestingly, our research has consistently shown that management style is a two-way process. That is, it not only deals with the amount of delegation downward, but also includes the atmosphere created to allow criticisms and conflicts to rise upward in the organization. To delegate authority for an action and then be unwilling to listen to the explanation that the resources allowed are not sufficient to accomplish the action does not create a delegative climate, but one of fear. Thus, when examining management style, one must look at the two aspects to understand how the process is operating.

Moreover, management style is another area where one cannot assume that the highest score is best. The basic mission of the organization must be considered. For example, in a research and development type of organization, a highly delegative environment is apt to promote the freest flow of ideas and greatest creativity, and therefore be "best." This same level of delegation in a mature and highly capital-intensive industry would probably be quite inefficient. Also, because different types of environments require differing management practices, it is not uncommon to find modification of the basic management style in various functional departments of an organization; for example, what is right for accounting is not necessarily right for marketing.

Thus, in management style, the goal is an amount of delegation appropriate to the jobs that must be accomplished. When this relationship is properly balanced, the organization receives the greatest amount of individual effort possible while maintaining a measure of control over what and how things get done. High delegation makes it doubly important that the climate aspects relating to individual and organizational goal clarity are also strong to provide the most effective framework in which individuals can channel their efforts.

Low scores can be a signal that people are frustrated and feel they do not have sufficient say in how results are achieved. In this case, it is appropriate to question whether management is more directive than is necessary for efficient operations.

Performance Orientation

Organizations differ in the nature of demands they place upon their members. In some, the focus is upon how a job is done, while in others it is upon the results produced. A results-focused orientation has several characteristics: people know what results are expected of them and the basis upon which their performance will be evaluated, and feel that they will be held accountable for their success or failure. Moreover, the emphasis is on high levels of performance, with goals and standards representing a challenge to those involved.

Low scores on this dimension may indicate that accountability is diffuse and indefinite, with no one being clearly responsible for producing specific results. When accountability is unclear, failure to accomplish the expected results may have little, if any, effect upon the individual responsible. In such cases, the failure is either ignored or rationalized as the result of uncontrollable factors. A finding that individuals are not held accountable is frequently a danger signal of a shortcoming in the organization's ability to tie individual performance to organizational objectives.

Organizations should strive to be reasonably high on this dimension, since over time a low score would indicate a tendency to tolerate less than competent performance. Too high a score, however, can indicate a tendency to emphasize only immediate, profit-producing activities, giving less than adequate attention to long-range, developmental actions. Thus a company with very high ratings should question whether the organization's focus is sufficiently broad to ensure a healthy future. Reference to the clarity dimension can help in this regard.

Organizational Vitality

Perceptions of vitality are important because they condition the mood or sense of esprit de corps within which people conduct their activities. In high-scoring organizations, people feel that the organization and its management will recognize and seize good opportunities as they arise. Because this dynamic nature implies a faster pace of activities, people expect to keep up with that pace. This is the type of environment generally preferred by competent, venturesome, achievement-oriented individuals. An organization interested in retaining highly talented, aggressive people should seek to be viewed as dynamic.

There are enterprises, however, that are best served by a perception of moderate vitality. Many mature, steady, or level-growth companies, for example, fall into this category. This kind of organization is designed to be relatively more prudent and cautious when responding to sudden events. It focuses upon the application of well-learned methods and know-how rather than aggressive behavior. Rather than encouraging extremely venturesome people, it needs those who are highly cooperative and unlikely to take risks. Such an organization will have modest or low scores on organizational vitality, scores that represent a relatively conservative approach. As such, a low score is likely to be a statement of fact, with things as they should be given the nature of the business, rather than an expression of dissatisfaction with the company's methods.

A number of other climate factors can contribute to low ratings of vitality. One of these is inadequate delegation, wherein people are insufficiently attuned to the problem-solving processes of the company. Perceptions of an overly cautious decision style will also contribute to ratings of low vitality. When people feel a lack of clarity of plans and goals, they will also tend to underestimate the organization's vitality. Low vitality, therefore, may be a reflection of other basic problems in the climate.

Compensation

Compensation is a key part of organizational climate because it reflects perceptions about the rewards available to and received by employees. The existence of multicompany survey data makes it possible for management to compare perceptions of reality with the actual levels of compensation.

High scores on this factor, which reflect satisfaction with the compensation system as a whole, can result from a belief in the compensation plan's competitiveness compared to other employers. It also reflects a belief in the system's internal equity, which means people believe that their work is compensated fairly relative to other jobs in the organization. However, a third element in the compensation factor warrants careful attention: the relationship of pay and rewards to performance. When high scores are recorded on this factor because compensation is seen as both equitable and competitive, management should also determine whether people see a close relationship between what they accomplish and the rewards they receive. This important compensation element may be overlooked in situations where most people are basically satisfied with their rewards.

Low scores suggest that people believe their compensation is low in comparison with what they think they could obtain elsewhere. If this perception is an accurate reflection of reality, management may, depending on its purposes, consider a revision of its compensation structure or salary administration. On the other hand, if objective comparisons indicate a good competitive position, communication to employees about compensation is probably inadequate and should be revised.

Another possible reason for low scores on this dimension is a feeling that groups or individuals within the organization do not receive equal compensation relative to their job responsibilities and their performance. This again can reflect a case where communication of salary policy is inadequate or where other communication or performance measurement problems cloud the ability of people to judge their compensation realistically. Low scores can, of course, also be indicative of very real inequities, in which case problems exist in the implementation phase of compensation policy.

Human Resource Development

Human resource development is one means by which organizations provide for their future success. In creating a climate conducive to the realization of individual potential, the company increases the possible contribution of individuals to the business. It therefore makes good business sense to be strong in this dimension.

Human resource development has several aspects. It involves the success of policies and programs, formal and informal, that develop people in their current positions and prepare them for positions of greater responsibility. In addition to preparing competent people who will seize those opportunities, it also involves the availability of the growth opportunities themselves.

Low scores on this dimension can arise from either of these areas. The most difficult to deal with is the situation in which a company is not expanding. In such situations, ratings on this dimension are probably low because of perceived limitations in developmental and promotional opportunities. However, only the company's management can answer the question, Is the lack of company growth inhibiting opportunities for personal growth, or is the company not growing because people are not encouraged to take on broader responsibilities and move in new directions?

Occasionally, situations arise in which the emphasis on individual development is misdirected and not in conformity with organizational objectives. Personal development per se is emphasized and developmental programs are not properly integrated with organizational plans. Very high scores on this dimension may indicate such a situation, particularly when other climate dimensions (for example, performance orientation, organization clarity) are not concomitantly high. However, while it is possible to be too high here, as a general rule this is a dimension where positive results are desirable.

Again, the results and possible corrective actions must be evaluated from the standpoint of the organization and its business environment, since these will influence the ability to provide the desired developmental opportunities.

Other Climate Dimensions

The eight dimensions discussed above are the ones that have emerged in study after study. Many other elements of an organization affect manager perceptions but are more specific to the particular company or issue being studied. As will be seen in some of the case studies presented in part III, these specific issues are also investigated through the survey format and help shed light on the impact of the standard dimensions.

6 Interpreting Climate Results

Interpreting the results of a climate survey requires consideration of the overall picture of the organization that emerges, of the interrelationships of the dimensions, of each dimension in itself, of individual questions within a dimension, and of differences across units or levels of the organization. The specific conclusions for an organization are determined by the complex patterns that emerge from this analysis in the context of that organization's particular situation—its industry, the desires of its leaders, the motivations of its people, and so on.

The dimension, rather than the item, level is usually the most effective at which to begin the analysis. The score on an individual dimension is interpreted first for what it conveys about the aspect of the organization's climate that it is measuring. Second, a more complete understanding of the climate is derived from the pattern of scores across the dimensions. Although the dimensions measure somewhat different elements of the climate, they are never totally independent of one another. For instance, neither conceptually nor in the measurement operation can the emphasis that an organization puts on results be totally separated from the clarity of its goals and plans. Because they are interrelated, one dimension can help explain or add meaning to the results in another.

Development of this overall picture is essential for understanding the survey findings, and becomes doubly important in determining what can or should be changed in the climate as a result of those findings. When steps to improve a particular area of climate are considered, attention must be given to the likelihood that other climate aspects will inhibit or enhance the success of these efforts.

A third step in the process is evaluation of each item in each dimension. In our own eight-dimension system, the items within each dimension are closely related to one another. By computing scores in percentiles, a type of standard score, we equate the averages and distributions of each item. The effect of these two actions is to determine that the scores on different items within a dimension will tend to be very similar for any organization. Thus, if a company scores at the seventieth percentile on the clarity of company goals, it will tend to score near the seventieth percentile on other items in the clarity dimension, such as the completeness of plans.

Because of this method of questionnaire construction, an additional diagnostic capability emerges from item variations within a dimension. Since the expectation is that each item will have approximately the same score, one or two that deviate widely from that score usually point to a specific set of circumstances within the organization. Sometimes these circumstances are easily explainable in light of the company's recent history, policies, or other factors. Often, however, such item deviations point directly to an aspect of the company's management processes that is out of balance with the others. Thus, an examination of item deviations within a dimension can be highly diagnostic.

A possible final step is to look for differences across divisions, units, or management levels. Possible climate differences among such units and levels may uncover specific problems. On the other hand, these differences may be appropriate and desirable. But the information must be isolated before it can be evaluated.

The case study presented below illustrates the process of examining climate results through analysis of an actual company using a very simple subunit categorization. Based on responses to questionnaires by fifty-three management personnel, it gives overall company results and findings for each of the eight dimensions, with comparative subunit analysis for only two management levels, the eight individuals who report directly to the vice president and general manager and the forty-five who have other reporting relationships. Functional units within the company and other management levels were not part of the study.

Note that overall results are presented first, since they provide a focus for understanding the role of the findings for each dimension and for the appropriate subunits. The company and subunit results are shown visually on percentile graphs which relate them to norms established on a wide range of other organizations.

Company Profiles—Alpha Corporation

Alpha is a functionally organized business engaged in a relatively narrow range of light manufacturing. It is a fairly autonomous division of a multibillion-dollar firm and represents one of that firm's diversifications into new product areas. While the technology involved is not as esoteric as some associated with the space age, the business still faces major technical problems in making its products more applicable to various mass markets.

As shown in the overall profile (figure 6-1), dimension scores for the Alpha Corporation are in some cases above the cross-company average (50th percentile) and in some cases below average. High ratings are obtained on decision-making (61st percentile), performance orientation (55th percentile), and organizational clarity (54th percentile), while lower than average ratings are obtained on compensation (45th percentile), human resource development (46th percentile), and management style (46th percentile).

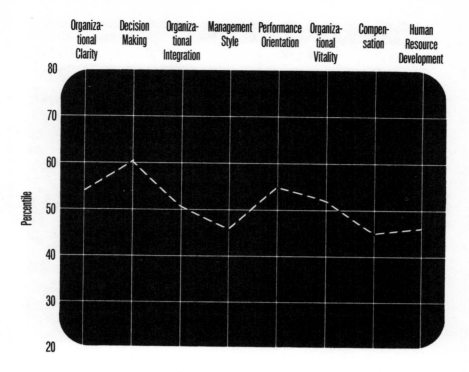

Figure 6-1. Alpha Corporation—Overall Company Results

This pattern is indicative of an organization with clear business objectives and a strong emphasis on performance at both the organizational and individual levels. In a relative sense, there is less concern for people than for business performance, as evidenced by the lower ratings in the people-management areas of compensation, development, and management style. These observations are discussed more fully below, under "Analysis of Results by Dimension."

The second profile chart (figure 6-2) compares the climate ratings given by managers reporting directly to the vice president and general manager with those of managers having other reporting relationships. The most striking aspect of the Alpha Corporation results is the relatively wide gap between these two levels. The top group is characterized by a profile that varies between the 61st and the 80th percentile, with high points on the decision-making and vitality factors and low points on compensation, human resource development, and clarity. The second level of management varies between the 43rd and the 59th percentile, with the highs on decision-making and performance orientation and the lows on compensation, human resource development, and management style.

Past research has indicated that a gap in climate scores between the few

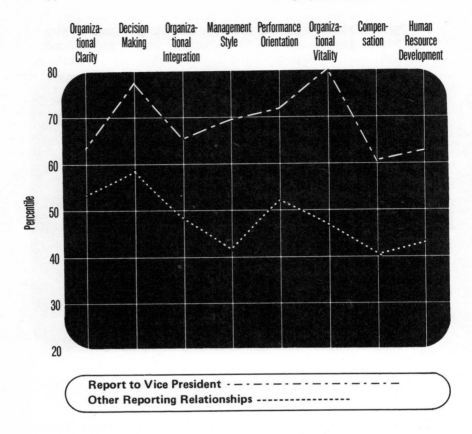

Figure 6-2. Alpha Corporation—Results by Reporting Level

people at the top of the organization and the bulk of management is a normal phenomenon. Across a large number of companies, this gap is normally eight to eighteen percentage points. But in this case, some of the differences are very striking, reaching thirty-two percentage points on organizational vitality and twenty-seven points on management style. Thus, while the climate perceived below the top is not entirely negative, it is certainly much less positive than that experienced by top management. On the other hand, the nature of the profile is similar. For instance, compensation and human resource development are seen as the least favorable aspects of the climate by both groups. It is the *level* at which these aspects are experienced, however, that is totally different for the two groups. The following analysis will look at each of the factors in turn, considering the individual items that entered into the factor scores.

Analysis of Results by Dimension

The following charts and commentary present each dimension and its related items from the survey. In each chart, the bars beside each item represent the percentile ratings given to that item by the two management levels in the company.

It is important in looking at the data to consider not only the position of the item relative to the data bank average, but also the position of the items relative to one another. As explained earlier, differences among items provides additional diagnostic information about relative strengths and weaknesses of the work environment.

Organizational Clarity. The Alpha Corporation is seen as having clear goals and defined plans to meet those goals (figure 6-3). The planning system is considered formal and relatively complete. Interestingly, top management sees the planning system as less formal than do lower levels. This may reflect the fact that

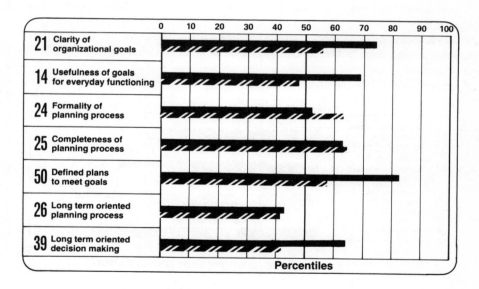

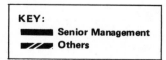

Figure 6-3. Alpha Corporation—Organizational Clarity

planning within Alpha is more a budgeting process than a true planning system. If so, top management would be aware of the lack of strategic planning, whereas lower levels might not be. This possibility is supported by the fact that planning is seen to be short-range by both levels of management. In all, however, the management appears to have a good understanding of the immediate objectives of the business and how it intends to meet them. If a problem exists, it is in developing a more long-range view of the directions that the business will take.

Decision-making. Decisions are viewed as being made on a reasonably informed basis and implemented and evaluated effectively (figure 6-4). The organizational structure is seen as quite viable and decision-making is regarded as being at appropriate levels. Thus, on clarity and decision-making, two of the most important elements of an effective organization, the Alpha Corporation appears to be well aligned for effective performance, especially as related to the short run. It might be noted, however, that on the issue of whether decisions are made at appropriate levels, an exceptionally large gap exists between top and middle-level management. This usually reflects a belief on the part of middle managers that greater operational decision-making can be delegated downward.

Organizational Integration. Integration, the communications and interrelationships among units in the company, is seen to be at an average level (figure 6-5).

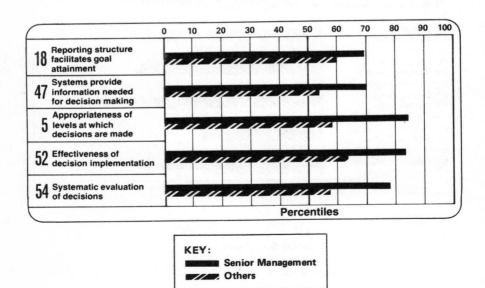

Figure 6-4. Alpha Corporation—Decision-Making

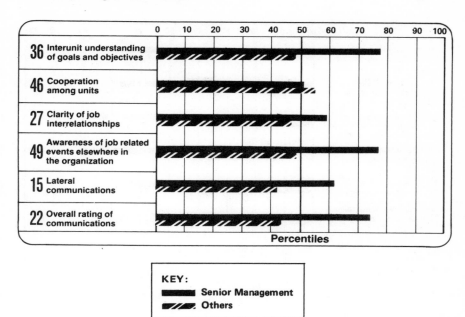

Figure 6-5. Alpha Corporation—Organizational Integration

Interestingly, top management rates interunit cooperation significantly lower than it does the other aspects of integration. In fact, this group scores lower on the cooperation item than does the middle management group. This result may indicate some problem in obtaining cooperation among the major units of the business, as headed by the members of the top management group. If cooperation cannot be obtained at this level, it is doubtful whether effective integration for major new programs or innovations can be achieved.

Management Style. The most significant aspect of the management style factor is the wide difference between the two management groups (figure 6-6). The lower-level group is fairly consistent in their responses, averaging close to the 42nd percentile. This group sees the management style as being somewhat restrictive of individual initiative and one in which upward communications are not encouraged. Top management's responses are much more differentiated. This group sees the management style as much more delegative, but they also see the organization as one in which conflicts are not openly discussed. This finding, coupled with the previous finding on interunit cooperation, would suggest that there is a need for greater trust and openness among members of top management. Significant unresolved conflicts appear to exist among this group.

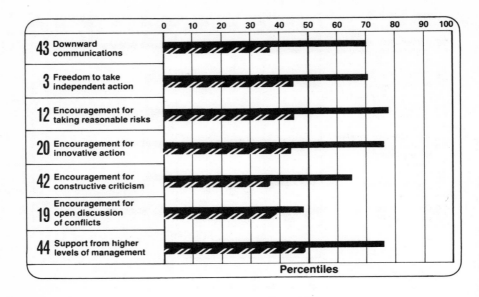

Figure 6-6. Alpha Corporation—Management Style

Performance Orientation. The Alpha Corporation is clearly one that has high performance expectations for its people (figure 6-7). The demands are seen as challenging, with the exact nature of these demands reasonably clear. Interestingly, the top management group perceives performance expectations as being exceptionally clear (82nd percentile), but quite a large gap exists between their perceptions and those of the other group (51st percentile). This latter group also perceives considerable demand for high levels of performance (60th percentile), which can lead to "wheel spinning" if the demand is not coupled with equivalent clarity. Thus, while the area does not appear to represent a critical problem, communication of performance expectations to the middle management group does appear to suffer some deficiencies.

Organizational Vitality. The vitality factor is the one that evidences the largest gap between the two management groups, with a spread of thirty-three percentage points on the total factor, which tends to be consistent across most of the items (figure 6-8). An exception to this trend is the forty-three point spread on the perceived "timeliness of decision-making." Top management sees

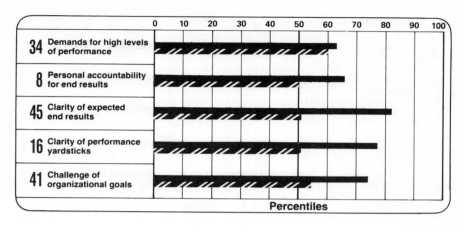

		0	10	20	30	40	50	60	70	80	90	100

34 **Demands for high levels of performance**

8 **Personal accountability for end results**

45 **Clarity of expected end results**

16 **Clarity of performance yardsticks**

41 **Challenge of organizational goals**

Percentiles

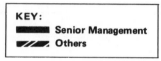

KEY:
▬▬ Senior Management
▰▰▰ Others

Figure 6-7. Alpha Corporation—Performance Orientation

decisions as being made in a very timely fashion, whereas those at lower levels see decisions as often being very delayed. This result is undoubtedly related to the earlier findings that showed that the middle management group believed that decisions could be made at lower levels and also believed that their freedom to act was somewhat limited. The implication here is that decisions are not being made close enough to the operating levels. Otherwise, middle management perceives the organization as being somewhat of a pacesetter in its industry, with an average amount of internal vitality.

Compensation. Compensation represents an area of negative feelings for the lower-level group (figure 6-9). At that level, satisfaction with compensation is low, related primarily to perceptions of internal inequities rather than low pay. Indeed, managers at this level score at the 36th percentile in their feelings of being paid fairly compared to others doing similar work *within* the company, whereas they are at the 48th percentile on their feelings of being paid fairly compared to people doing similar work *outside* the company. They also feel that there is a weak relationship between performance and compensation. The top management group, on the other hand, is quite satisfied with their compensation, with little differentiation in their feelings toward competitiveness or equity.

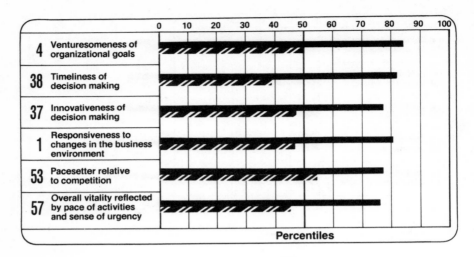

Figure 6-8. Alpha Corporation—Organizational Vitality

Human Resource Development. The organization is seen as being moderately successful in developing people from within for higher-level jobs (figure 6-10). There is a feeling, however, that promotion opportunities are quite limited, and that even where opportunities exist, the scope of the search for talent within the company is also quite limited. This latter feeling comes from the middle-level managers and contrasts sharply with that of the top management group, which feels that there is a very wide search when opportunities for promotion exist. This contrast may indicate that the problem lies more in communications than in the procedures for talent search. The items indicating lower-than-average job challenge and person-job match may indicate a problem of low commitment and motivation. With perceptions of high performance demands and relatively low opportunities for personal growth, the company faces the risk of losing some of the more talented middle managers.

Summary of Alpha Findings

The Alpha Corporation is one which has a very businesslike orientation to its management. Actions are planned and decisions are made carefully and followed

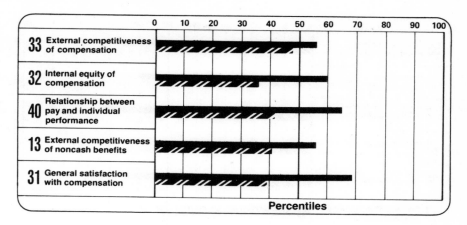

Figure 6-9. Alpha Corporation—Compensation

up aggressively. The company is tightly run insofar as the demands are high and the expectations are laid out clearly. Within this system, however, delegation beyond the top management group is somewhat limited. Thus, below top management, people see their roles primarily as carrying out well-formulated plans, rather than as innovating in any major way. Morale, while not extremely low, is less than average. This attitude appears to be due primarily to the feelings of constraint, coupled with the view that opportunities for advancement are very limited and that compensation is not determined equitably.

These middle management perceptions contrast very sharply with those of top management. Within this latter group, there is a very high level of satisfaction and commitment. The one area that does seem to be a problem among this group is that of open communication and cooperation. In very sharp contrast with their perceptions of other aspects of the climate, these people feel that basic conflicts receive little discussion and that cooperation among the major units of the company is somewhat limited.

Thus, three areas seem to require management attention. One is the encouragement of the top management group to work as a team, including the willingness to address sensitive issues that may be involved in facilitating cooperation. The second is in delegating greater decision-making latitude to operating levels. There seems to be a strong message from middle management that too many issues must be referred to the executive group and decisions are

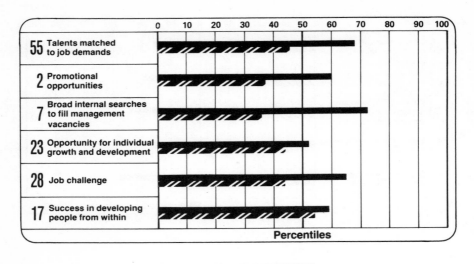

Figure 6-10. Alpha Corporation—Human Resource Development

slow in being reached. This perception may well be related to conflicts within that group, or it may just represent the historical style of the organization. In either event, accountabilities can be reexamined to determine where the company could profitably push down decision-making.

The third area is somewhat of a morale problem among middle management. Here the problem is maintaining the personal commitment that will produce sustained high levels of performance. The problem, which seems to center around compensation and career development (including the opportunity to exercise more individual initiative), can have a variety of solutions, depending upon the facts behind the perceptions. For instance, we have often found cases wherein compensation was perceived as noncompetitive when in reality it was highly competitive. In such cases, communication is more important than changes in the compensation structure. On the other hand, if an objective analysis indicates that this group is paid neither equitably nor competitively, it would be incumbent upon the company to take aggressive steps to correct the situation.

The problem of career development usually presents more complicated challenges, but here also perceptions must be evaluated against the facts, and communication of problems must be evaluated against the quality and effects of the programs themselves. Does an effective manpower planning and development program exist for middle management? What are the projected needs for higher-level managers over the next five to ten years? Do opportunities exist to assign more accountability to the incumbents of some of these jobs in order to prepare them for future opportunities? In examining the answers to these questions, the Alpha Corporation can lay the foundation for significant improvements in morale and commitment of its middle management. The very disparate results on vitality indicate that the upper level of management has not effectively transmitted its basic enthusiasm about the business to lower levels. This is especially significant since the company is putting a great deal of effort into perfecting new products with very significant market potential.

Summary

This case illustrates the technique by which climate data are examined. The overall profile provides a sense of the company's style—the qualities it emphasizes and those it does not. An item-by-item examination illuminates some of the possible causes and dynamics behind these characteristics. Finally, examining the demographic categorizations (in this case, management level) provides further insight into how the organization is operating hierarchically, functionally, or across time. The following chapter elaborates further on various demographic patterns of management climate.

7 Climate Trends Within an Organization

As the Alpha example illustrates, when climate is translated down and across an organization, it often undergoes subtle changes created by individual styles and organizational roles. This phenomenon can be seen through examining climate results by management level and by functional or profit center units. Even though the main outlines of a particular company's climate are generally discernible among its components, many specific aspects change quite significantly. Contrasting the results of these components often yields insights not apparent in the overall company results.

Results by Management Levels

Analysis of results by management levels provides information regarding perception of the intended climate at lower levels. As noted in chapter 6, top management tends to perceive climate more favorably than do those below. This finding in itself is not surprising, because the leaders have had personal success in the organization and direct involvement in important decision-making. However, differences across units or levels may be quite revealing to the senior management group.

Figure 7-1 contrasts the seven vice presidents with the other managers in an actual organization. The basic climate pattern is similar in the two management groups, but as with the Alpha Corporation, a very significant difference exists in the overall levels of the ratings. This difference is generally greater than that found in the "average" company, as shown by the shaded area in figure 7-1. In this particular situation, a new CEO had worked very intensely with the top management team for a few months, but the influence of the efforts had not yet been felt below that level.

In a second company (figure 7-2), the climate at the top is not only different from that which exists below, but in some respects less favorable. Here the senior management group perceives problems of a strategic nature, seeing organizational goals and plans as unclear and the decision-making structure as failing to facilitate accomplishment of organizational objectives. While this result reflects a serious problem at the top, the situation does not seem to have had as negative an impact on the operating levels. Either top management is reflecting problems oriented primarily toward the future or its present confusion in priorities has not yet made itself felt below. In either event, results of this type

55

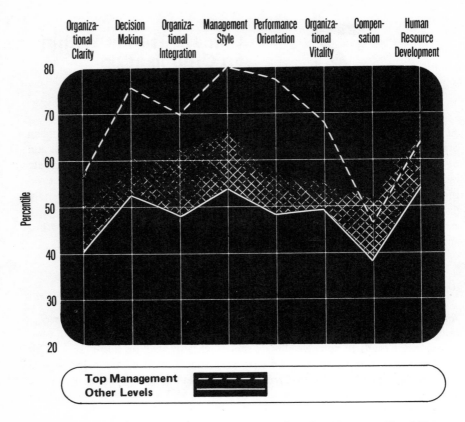

Figure 7-1. An Example of Similar Profiles with a Gap Between Top Management and Other Reporting Levels

should provide a strong impetus for top management to address itself to its own understanding o the organization's directions.

Results by Organizational Units

Just as climate changes as it is translated through successive layers of management, it also changes as messages are sent and implemented across various organizational units. Figures 7-3 and 7-4 present two examples of this type of analysis. Both organizations have units engaged in similar business activities at different geographic locations.

The climate profiles of two operating divisions in a utility company display a great deal of similarity (figure 7-3). In this case, a combination of the nature of the business, style of its leaders, and strength of its management processes and tradition all combine to create an overall climate that seems to have had a strong

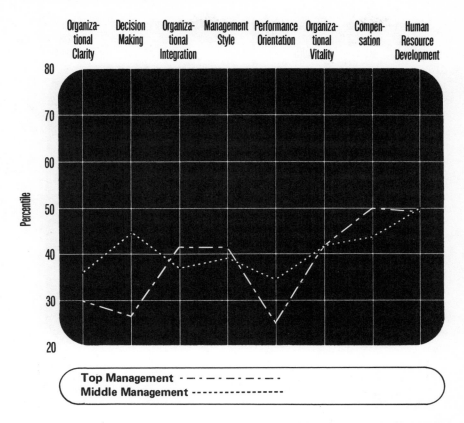

Figure 7-2. An Example of Dissimilar Profiles Between Management Levels

influence on the climate in these units. Interestingly, one of the greatest differences is in management style. Thus, despite a relatively pervasive overall climate, sufficient latitude exists for each general manager to affect the extent of delegation within his unit.

There is little to suggest that the units of a second company (figure 7-4) are part of the same organization. Each of these units seems quite different from the next, despite the fact that they are part of the same company. In this case, the influence of top management on the operating climates is minimal, the company being more in the mode of a conglomerate.

Staff-Line Differences

The effect a manager's position and job responsibilities can have on his view of the climate is illustrated by comparing the climate perceptions of managers in staff positions and of those in line positions.

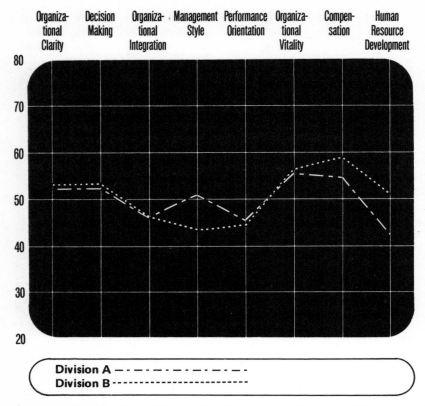

Figure 7-3. An Example of Similar Profiles for Two Operating Divisions in the Same Company

A line unit is defined as any group engaged in the primary business activities of the enterprise, usually designing, building, and distributing the company's products or services. Staff units are those engaged in providing services to the rest of the organization. Staff units usually include personnel, finance, accounting, business planning, management information systems or data processing, and general administration. On the average, staff positions represent about 10 to 20 percent of the climate survey sample in any given organization.

As indicated in figure 7-5, staff managers perceive their organization's climate less favorably than do line managers in all areas except compensation. The areas in which the largest differences occur between line and staff are in performance orientation and organizational clarity. The climate data support the view that the nature of staff positions may make clear definition of expected results more difficult. Performance in these jobs is often more difficult to measure in even the most sophisticated performance measurement system

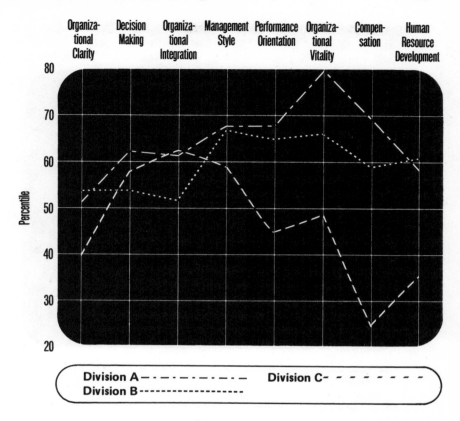

Figure 7-4. An Example of Dissimilar Profiles for Three Operating Divisions in the Same Company

because of the lack of readily quantifiable objectives.

Staff managers feel equally accountable as do line managers for their results, but have less clarity about what is expected of them and how their performance will be measured. Despite feeling equally or more satisfied with their compensation than line managers, staff people see less relationship between pay and performance, quite possibly because of this lack of clear performance standards and measures.

Lower ratings of organizational clarity may also reflect a peculiarity of the staff assignments. As integrators or coordinators in the organization, staff managers normally are in a position to see plans that are not coordinated or goals that conflict. Where organizational goals and plans lack completeness or are communicated poorly, the impact on staff people as a group is apt to be more apparent.

In summary, lower ratings of climate are not uncommon across staff units

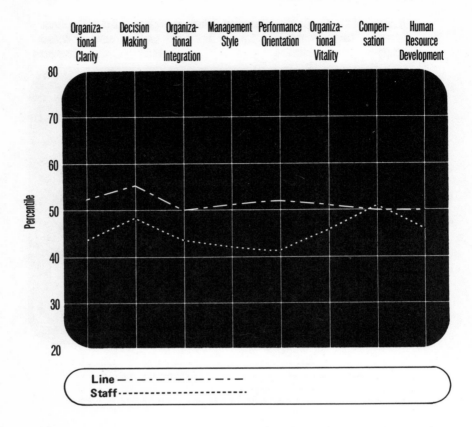

Figure 7-5. Climate Profile for Line and Staff Groups

of an organization. However, while a general trend exists for combined staff functions across a variety of organizations, it by no means occurs in all situations. Moreover, as with other cross-company climate patterns, its existence elsewhere does not lessen the potential problems it might reflect in a given organization.

8 The "Right" Climate

As we indicated previously, no pattern of climate scores can be considered ideal, and no one climate is "right" for all organizations. Determination of the appropriate climate depends on a number of highly complex issues which resist imposition of absolute external standards. Instead, any management climate must be judged on the pragmatic criterion of how well it helps the organization achieve its objectives. In actuality, what is a good climate for one company may be completely unsuitable for the next.

Different types of industries produce different types of climates. Ordinarily, a given organization must examine itself in terms of its own missions and challenges as well as those of its industry if it is to determine what climate is best for it, and therefore what climate it must strive to achieve.

A high or low percentile for every dimension or item is not necessarily good or bad. What benefits one company does not always help another, depending on the industry, the company's stage of development, its mission, and other factors. Therefore, a desire to be high on all climate factors is probably misguided. For example, a firm such as an electric utility with a large capital investment and an overriding requirement for reliability would probably require more centralized control than a multiproduct, consumer-oriented firm that deals in highly volatile markets.

Despite the need to emphasize the distinct aspects of each organization's climate, some common denominators do exist for organizations within a certain industry, for organizations stressing certain goals, and for the majority of organizations in general. Research designed to determine whether such common denominators exist has produced a number of significant conclusions, several of which will be discussed below. Findings such as these help present the management of a company with a picture of what exists, what is typical, and what is possible. Only a consideration of these elements can lead to a description of what is best for a particular company.

Climate Relationships Among Organizations

The first step to seeking generalizations about climate was to learn whether companies have distinct climate profiles and whether units within a company have distinct profiles—that is, whether management climate is consistent throughout a company, or whether individual differences in perceptions and rating tendencies overshadow the influence of top management. To answer these questions, two hypotheses were formulated:

Companies are sufficiently different from one another so that their climate profiles will be unrelated.

The influence of top management upon a company's climate will cause different units within a company to have similar profiles.

The results of the research strongly supported these hypotheses, as shown in figure 8-1. The correlations between pairs of companies range from −.88 to +.97, with a median of +.05, which is not significantly different from zero.[1] In fact, the actual data fall surprisingly close to a random distribution, one that could be obtained by tossing coins. In contrast, the correlations among units

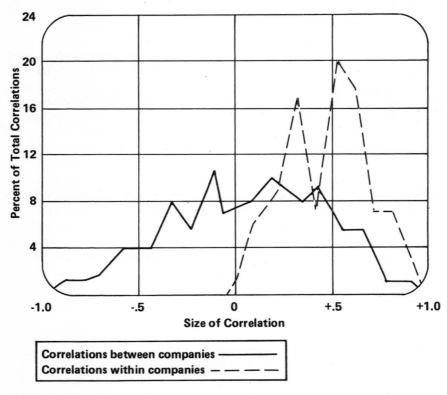

Source: Reprinted from G. Gordon, B. Goldberg, "Is There a Climate for Success" *Management Review*, May 1977 (New York: AMACOM, a division of American Management Associations, 1977), p. 39.

Figure 8-1. Correlations of Climate Profiles Between and Within Companies

within companies show a very striking departure from a random distribution. Here the results range from −.04 to +.84, with a median of +.54. Obviously, variability exists in how closely units within a company resemble one another in climate, but the tendency is for a very substantial relationship.

Climate and Results

With the overall consistency of climate within an organization established, the next stage of the research attempted to find relationships between a company's climate and the results it achieves. For this study, results were defined as the five-year average annual rate of growth in net income (compound growth rate), because this measure recognizes profit, improvement, and long-range achievement. In addition, this measure also reflects a development over time appropriate to the three to five years usually required for climate change. The study sought common climate dimensions in companies with high rates of growth.

The findings revealed that companies with such successful performance are clearly similar on some climate dimensions and dissimilar on others. Organizational clarity, organizational integration, and compensation show a much greater correlation to performance than do the other dimensions (figure 8-2). High-growth companies develop clear objectives and pursue them through a well-understood planning system, with communication that integrates the efforts of units to achieve goals. The high compensation levels may be explained by one of two possibilities: companies doing well pay well, or companies that pay well demand high performance for what they pay. Surprisingly, performance orientation does not have a statistically significant relationship to performance results, nor does management style.

Further analysis delineated and evaluated items within the dimensions according to their relationship to performance. Although the relationships vary, a number of items have a significant connection with profit:

1. The organization has clear goals.
2. The organization has defined plans to meet its goals.
3. The planning system is formal.
4. Planning is comprehensive.
5. Information for decision-making is available.
6. Information for decision-making is used.
7. Good lateral communications exist.
8. Overall communications are good.
9. Units understand each other's objectives.
10. Clear measures of managerial performance exist.
11. Managers are clear about the results expected of them.
12. Benefits are competitive.
13. Compensation is related to performance.

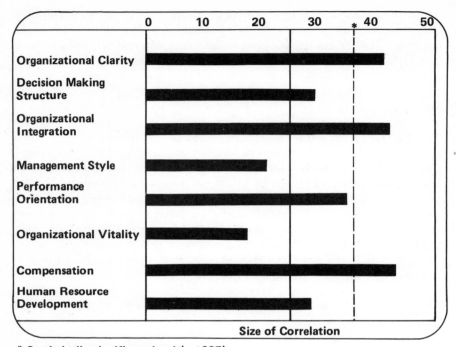

Source: Reprinted from G. Gordon, B. Goldberg, "Is There a Climate for Success" *Management Review*, May 1977 (New York: AMACOM, a division of American Management Associations, 1977), p. 40.

Figure 8-2. Correlations Between Climate Dimensions and Five-Year Growth in Net Profit

Many of these items share an implication of clarity through communications and accessibility of information. For example, the compensation and performance orientation items indicate a clear understanding of what constitutes performance. A company with successful results identifies objectives, plans for their accomplishment, and measures performance, all with widespread communication of relevant information. Thus, the overriding implication appears to be that successful companies are best at marshaling relevant information and disseminating it to the places where it can be appropriately used in operating the organization.

Climate, Morale, and Performance Demand

Morale has very often been confused with productivity, but abundant research has demonstrated that the relationship between the two is far from direct.[2] On the other hand, it is common wisdom that the greater the pressure for results that is put on someone, the better those results will be. Needless to say, this "truism" is also false. Rather, both morale and performance demand, when coupled with proper organization, communications, training, supervision, and so on, will certainly yield more positive results. Alone, neither creating an atmosphere of demand nor personal satisfaction are unique keys to performance. It is important, however, to understand how each of these elements fits within the overall climate and therefore its potential contribution to success.

To explore these relationships, we looked at approximately 100 companies that had participated in management climate surveys and used essentially the same questionnaire. Table 8-1 presents the ten items most highly correlated with items on satisfaction and performance demand.[3] Very obviously, what might produce a very satisfying work environment does not appear to be the same thing that produces a highly demanding one. Indeed, among the top ten items, only one is common to both areas; under both, people perceive the environment as having high vitality, reflected in a sense of urgency and a rapid pace of activities. Thus, when people are doing work that has an important and immediate purpose for the organization, they feel both a sense of demand to produce and a sense of satisfaction in performing their jobs. This may well explain why in "fat" organizations—those that seem to have more staff than they need—we have rarely noted a strong sense of esprit or motivation to achieve.

What makes a work environment a demanding one? The extent to which the company is seen as expecting high levels of performance from its managers is associated with

1. A clear sense of direction, reflected in clear company goals, which are seen to be challenging and a useful tool for everyday management. A complete planning process results in well-defined plans designed to accomplish those goals.
2. People with a clear definition of their authority who are held personally accountable for their achievements. If the measures of performance are

Table 8-1
Climate Items Most Related to Demand and Satisfaction

Demand	Satisfaction
Overall vitality	Overall vitality
Goal clarity	Opportunities for personal growth
Goal challenge	Emphasis placed on development from within
Goal utility	Talents matched to jobs
Completeness of planning	Overall communications
Existence of defined plans	Information available for decisions
Clarity of authority limits	Interunit cooperation
Personal accountability	Decisions made at appropriate levels
Clarity of performance yardsticks	Decisions implemented effectively
Constructive criticism encouraged	Few problems of internal management

clear, it is evident whether or not a goal has been achieved. Furthermore, the atmosphere is one in which constructive criticism is encouraged, rather than one in which mistakes are swept under the rug.

Thus, a demanding environment is not necessarily that in which over-whelming pressure is applied or people are seen as highly expendable. Rather, demand is seen to exist when a strong spotlight is placed upon performance— *defining the objectives, developing plans to meet them, and holding individuals accountable to carry out the plans.* One almost gets a feeling of "no place to hide." The organization has taken pains to assure that each individual has an identifiable role in contributing to its objectives, so that no one is overlooked in an atmosphere of confusion. In short, a demanding environment is one in which everyone has a job to do and in which it is easy to tell whether or not he is doing it.

These key attributes of a demanding environment contrast quite sharply with the major elements of a satisfying one. Here, the emphasis is not so much on organizational performance, but seems to have more of a flavor of satisfying personal needs. In particular, a satisfying environment is most characterized by

1. An emphasis placed upon developing human resources. Care is given to assure that the right people are in the right jobs and are being readied for the next job.
2. People who know what is going on and feel included. Communications are good, managers do not have to make decisions in states of high uncertainty, and other people are willing to cooperate when help is needed.
3. Management processes that work smoothly. The right people make the decisions, they are implemented, and there are few problems with the process.

This very positive picture certainly seems to depict a series of desirable organizational characteristics. However, whereas a demanding environment seems to focus on accomplishment, the major focus here appears to be on the process rather than on the result. That is, paying attention to people's careers and providing them with a great deal of information are actions that can help the organization thrive, but are much more removed from the central purposes of the organization than are setting objectives, planning for accomplishment, and measuring the results.

Even in the area of decision-making, there is almost a feeling that the process, in terms of adhering to the hierarchy (made at appropriate levels) and avoiding conflict (few problems), is as important as the quality of the decisions themselves. The entire set of attributes related to satisfaction can be interpreted as those things that will provide personal comfort to the individual, but will not necessarily encourage maximum contribution to the organization's purposes.

This is not to say that an organization can ignore the satisfaction of its employees at any level, for to do so would surely lead to performance decrements through loss of motivation and commitment. Retention of talented managers would be very difficult if they saw no opportunities for personal growth or if they saw the organization run in a truly chaotic manner. Yet if one were to build programs to try to maximize satisfaction, the results could well be deleterious to the organization, since they would tend not to include those elements that foster a feeling of high performance demand. Thus a balance is required, and fortunately the results indicate that a high vitality climate characterized by a sense of purpose and rapid pace of activities is conducive to feelings of both demand and satisfaction.

Climate Ratings and Organizational Differences

Although apparent guidelines emerged from the previous studies, they only reveal composite patterns that exist across a number of organizations judged successful in one way or another. They cannot be applied automatically as desired climate goals for any single company. Scores and comparative ratings on the climate dimensions cannot be considered ends in themselves. Even though managements are often anxious to see how their climate rates relative to others and whether their scores are high or low, a study of two actual companies, here called simply A and B, illustrates that climate analysis must go beyond the mere rating concept to provide meaningful, constructive information. Figure 8-3 presents the climate profiles of the two companies.

Company A is a manufacturer engaged primarily in one product area and having over $1 billion in annual revenues. From the relative high and low points of the climate profile, as well as the items included in the dimensions, the company can be characterized as a purposeful one which has implemented good systems and procedures for assuring efficient operation of the business. Methods of setting goals and developing plans at the individual and organizational levels provide managers with the clarity necessary to channel their efforts effectively. The company is seen as having systems that foster good communications and modes of interaction across units and provide the information necessary for decision-making.

The climate is a demanding one in which managers feel they will be held accountable for achieving high levels of performance and meeting well-defined goals. Although the management style is not considered to be highly delegative, individuals find their assignments challenging and see ample opportunity for ongoing growth and development. However, despite its clear plans and procedures, the company is viewed as lacking vitality because of its cautious manner of reacting to changes in the business environment rather than taking innovative, long-term approaches to future planning.

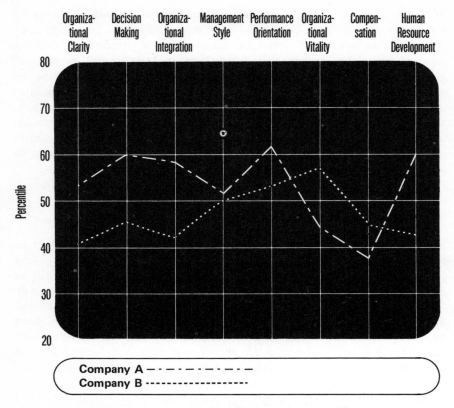

Figure 8-3. Comparison of Two Company Profiles

Although this analysis has provided quantitative indicators of the relative "strengths" and "weaknesses" of the climate, a broad perspective is needed to evaluate whether the so-called strengths are indeed positive and the so-called weaknesses negative. For example, one cannot assume that Company A should be higher in vitality, because it might make good business sense for the enterprise to be a conservative follower rather than an innovative leader in its field. On the other hand, the analysis may have pinpointed a weakness of which top management was not aware.

An example of a climate element probably not intended by management is the very low compensation ratings. Organizations vary considerably in the resources available for and philosophy toward compensation, but few, if any, want their employees to feel underpaid. In Company A, people do consider themselves underpaid. Although they feel salaries within the company suit the level of job responsibilities, they see little relationship between pay and performance, and they feel compensation and benefits are well below those of other organizations. Thus, the company's compensation system does not fulfill its role as a motivator of individual performance, despite an otherwise very challenging and purposeful climate.

In Company B, compensation is also viewed as inadequate, but other elements of the company's climate make it a very different situation from that of Company A. Managers in Company B perceive little clarity in the future plans and goals of the enterprise, and thereby do not understand how they can best contribute to the organization's and their own future success. Nonetheless, the climate is demanding in that individuals feel they will be held to a strict accounting for the results of their work. Because people sense an emphasis on strong levels of individual performance, the performance orientation rating is relatively high. However, the rating of this dimension is lower than that of Company A because one aspect, the defining of clear expected results is not seen to exist in Company B.

Additional insights into the two companies may be gained by examining ratings of individual items within the other dimensions as well. For example, the individual item results for Company B under management style (figure 8-4) indicate encouragement of a great deal of individual action and risk-taking, but not of the airing of conflicts to the same extent. More important, while the climate encourages risk, it does not convey a sense that top management will provide support when needed. These findings are consistent with other climate

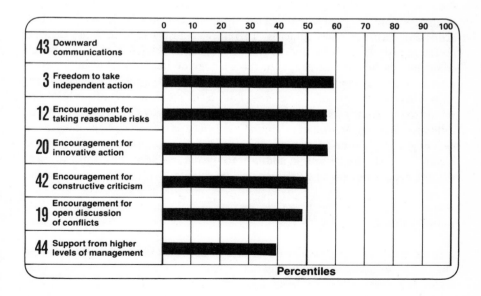

Figure 8-4. Company B—Management Style Results

elements for the company which reveal an impetus toward high individual performance but lack of formal or informal processes to assure that activities are directed adequately or results rewarded appropriately.

From the standpoint of the individual manager of Company B, such a climate is seen as very insecure, but high in vitality. The company's past actions and business results provide a clear explanation for this pattern. As a miniconglomerate, the company acquired and subsequently wrote off or sold numerous businesses over the past ten years. Thus, while being very dynamic and venturesome in its activities, it does not appear to have a clear sense of mission. The internal conflicts created within management by this unhealthy combination has been accompanied by unsatisfactory business results.

The comparison of these two companies underscores the fact that climate cannot be viewed in a vacuum and the results automatically interpreted as positive or negative. For example, in Company A, organizational vitality was viewed as low, while in Company B, it was considered quite high. However, the evidence makes it clear that Company B is not a more effective organization. Neither is there any evidence that Company A would benefit significantly from higher scores on this dimension. Climate analysis becomes an action-oriented tool only when the results are considered in light of the missions and structures of a given enterprise and are then translated into strategies, structure, processes, or people.

Any organization attempting to determine what climate is right for it must examine itself in terms of the missions and challenges of its industry as well as those that are uniquely its own. The data available indicate that different industries tend to produce somewhat different climates because of common needs and historical developments. Therefore, industry climate data provide a useful yardstick to help understand the consistent challenges faced by all companies within an industry, even though they do not indicate what is correct or appropriate in any single organization. On one hand, a given industry pattern may reflect the nature of the business, but on the other, it may reflect historical trends that are largely irrelevant today. Rather than providing a standard to be followed, industry information can be used most effectively as one element in deciding upon an organization's appropriate climate. Industry data offer a second level of comparison, in addition to overall management norms, to assist the individual company in evaluating its own climate.

Industry Profiles

Despite similarities in products or services or in size and location, organizations' climate, as we have seen, are influenced by many individual variables, such as the styles and personalities of leaders, organizational structure, and history and growth pattern. However, at least on some limited aspects, the climate results for organizations engaged in similar lines of business seem to be differentiated from others.

The profiles displayed in figure 8-5 represent some tentative data on industries currently represented in our data bank: manufacturing, banking, insurance, utilities, and retail businesses, restaurants, and hotels. The solid lines are the average of the companies we have studied within each industry. The shaded area represents the standard error of that average, a statistic that provides an estimate of the boundaries within which two thirds of the companies in the industry would be expected to fall. These profiles represent early trends, based upon a very limited number of companies; thus, they are more suggestive than definitive at this time. The data will produce more conclusive results as the numbers of companies increase.

Since manufacturing firms represent a conglomerate of a number of different types of businesses, it is not surprising to find little deviation of any single factor from the overall average, since different types of firms tend to cancel one another out on individual factors. Also, since manufacturing represents the bulk of the data base from which percentiles are computed, the average profile would of necessity be very close to the fiftieth percentile. There is, however, a significant trend for manufacturing firms to be lower on the human resource dimension than they are on the others. Compared to other businesses, manufacturing appears to be a little less people-oriented.

The profiles of insurance companies tend to be lower than those for other companies, that is, below the fiftieth percentile. While this result may reflect the particular companies surveyed, the more important aspect of the industry profile is the consistent relationship that can be observed among the eight climate dimensions. Attention to the financial needs of managers appears to be strong in insurance companies, while attention to specifying and measuring performance expected of individuals and the total organization is considerably weaker. Given the intensifying problems the industry has had to face in recent years, we have found widespread interest in putting more focus on performance, but a lack of history and current skill to accomplish this quickly.

Banking also shows a profile that is lower than average, but looking at the scores in relation to one another, decision-making is a relative high point, while a clear sense of direction seems to be especially low. The process of lending money is a highly systematic, information-based, decision-making activity, but is not necessarily related directly to strategic planning. Thus, one can understand the relatively positive perceptions of decision-making and the considerably lower ratings of clarity. Given numerous changes in federal law concerning banking and the appearance of entirely new competition from other types of financial enterprises, it is not surprising to find a low sense of clarity in this group. Finally, relatively limited delegation and encouragement of innovation exists, again a characteristic it is not surprising to find in banking.

The combination retail, restaurant, and hotel profile is very varied across

MANUFACTURING (N=58)

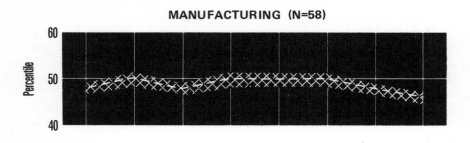

BANKING (N=10)

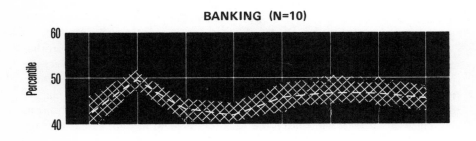

INSURANCE (N=10)

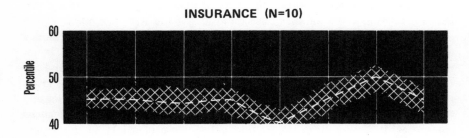

factors, yet for such a small sample of companies is highly consistent from company to company. Integration, delegation, and compensation are the low points of the profile. Performance orientation and vitality are high, along with clarity and decision-making. Retail organizations have the external image of

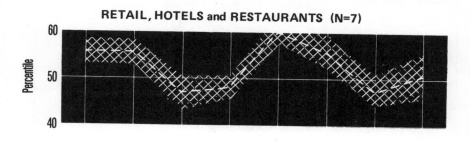

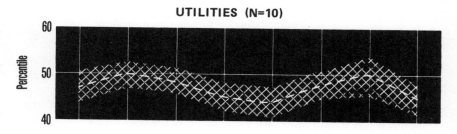

Figure 8-5. Industry Profiles

being low-paying companies that demand a great deal from their employees. The perceptions of internal management seem to confirm that image. Furthermore, the mission of these companies appears to be straightforward, without allowing a great deal of freedom to act to cloud the issues.

Utilities reveal certain internal similarities which set them apart from organizations engaged in other lines of business. Figure 8-6 is taken from a more intensive study of utility climates and shows responses of utility managers to specific questions on integration and clarity. As perceived by their managers, utilities tend to devote considerable attention to enhancing cooperation among units and creating channels for information to flow across the organization. Because the close relationship of generation and transmission demands integrated operations, companies have responded by providing the type of information systems and communications channels needed to assure reliable service. Thus, at the operating level, utilities have succeeded in creating a climate that

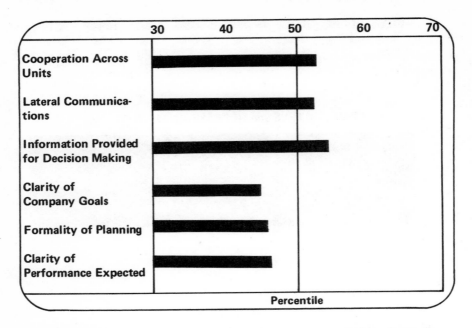

Figure 8-6. Utility Scores on Integration and Clarity

enables managers to focus efforts effectively upon problems or projects that go beyond the boundaries of individual departments or divisions.

However, these utilities have not been able to achieve the same focus at the strategic level. Compared to managers in other industries, utility managers are less clear about company goals and plans. Further, companywide planning is seen as less formal than that of the general business community. While solid tactical planning may exist in specific areas, such as contingency power supply, comprehensive corporate planning seems to have received less attention. However, the high degree of integration necessary in utilities makes the establishment and communication of a firm sense of direction more critical in this than in most other industries.

Utilities appear to share a climate in which there is a high concern for people and low concern for performance (figure 8-7). Perceptions of the competitiveness of compensation are high, with a resulting strong satisfaction with compensation. This evaluation may reflect a view of pay relative to the demands of the job rather than the amount of pay in the abstract. Compared to other managers, those in utilities feel pay is less closely tied to job performance and that their jobs are less challenging. This conclusion probably relates to the

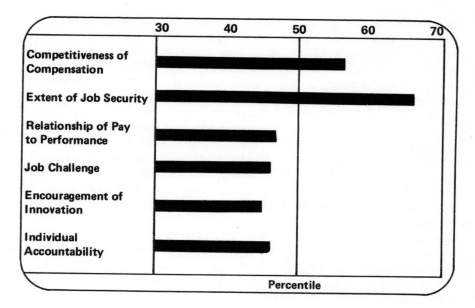

Figure 8-7. Utility Scores on Management of Human Resources

fact that they sense less encouragement to innovate and feel that they are held less personally accountable for the results they produce.

These findings raise the question of whether the climate in these utilities will serve for the future. The many unknowns in terms of fuels, the pressures of consumers and government, and the possibility of long-term alternatives to traditional utilities make for a demanding external environment. Utilities will need clear direction for change, innovative and talented individuals to bring it about, and an internal environment that supports dynamic managers. To achieve this condition, utilities will be able to look not to their past practices, but to those of more aggressive organizations in other sectors of the economy.

This study of utilities climate makes it clear that industry climate data do not merely provide a model for organizations in that industry to emulate, especially when industry-wide problems exist. In such cases, other standards of climate must be sought.

Job Security

Although it is not one of the eight major dimensions of climate, job security provides a useful perspective from which to compare the climate existing within industries and among companies. Thus, we customarily ask managers to evaluate how much security their organization offers its management. From our experience with perceptions of job security in numerous organizations, we have concluded that the issue surrounding security is not one of how much is good in absolute terms as much as it is a question of finding a level of job security appropriate to the needs of the business and of its people.

The effect of the nature of the business on the amount of security offered is suggested in figure 8-8, which presents the perceived level of job security by respondents in different industries. Utility companies are seen as offering the greatest amount of security, and retail and, strangely, banking the least. The utilities' need for stability and reliability has fostered higher job security compared to retail firms, which must constantly react to changes in public values, styles, habits, and geographic characteristics. Banking, which has decreased from earlier measures, has traditionally been thought of as a high-security industry.[4] However, with other types of financial firms entering traditional banking businesses, government opening the field to greater competition, and electronics creating a revolution in operations, managers may well have a sense of insecurity for the future. Therefore, job security must be considered in the context of the overall organizational and business climate.

A climate that meets the security needs of its manager seems to be more favorable than one in which security is felt to be either too low or too high.[5] In organizations where the managers see job security as being at about the right level, not only are the overall climate profiles higher, but long-term business

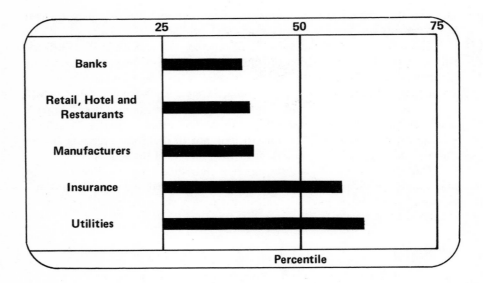

Figure 8-8. Perceived Job Security by Industry

performance has been better. The companies in which job security was considered to be adequate had higher average five-year growth rates in net income than those in which security was seen as insufficient or excessive. (Climate profiles for three different types of security orientations are presented in figure 8-9.)

In some organizations, job security is not an issue; that is, whether present job security is at the thirty-fifth percentile or the sixty-fifth, it is not far from where managers feel it should be. This type of climate is characterized by a balance between concern for the individual and concern for organizational performance. In this climate profile, organizational clarity, performance orientation, compensation, and human resource development are rated at above average levels. Managers feel that demands placed upon them are high and that these demands are accompanied by well-defined performance measures and clear goals and plans for the overall enterprise. They also feel that they are compensated

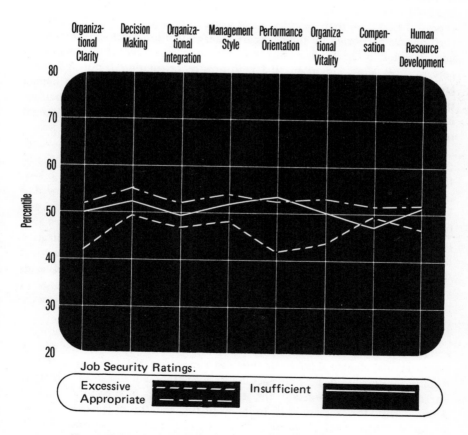

Figure 8-9. Climate Profiles for Different Security Patterns

fairly and are provided good opportunity for career development and pro-motion.

Ratings of management style are also quite high in this group, indicating that managers sense a good deal of freedom to accomplish their jobs in the most efficient manner. The overall impression conveyed by this profile is of an organization structured to accomplish well-defined ends, but allowing the freedom and delegation to facilitate individual contributions and their recogni-tion. That is, the demands are clear and high, but so are the potential rewards.

The climate in which managers feel that security is ten or more percentage points below where they believe it should be also receives generally favorable percentile ratings, but tends to place a great deal of emphasis on individual performance, with less attention to providing rewards for that performance. The highest-rated climate factors in this composite profile are decision-making and performance orientation. Management processes enable managers to know what is expected of them, provide them with the necessary decision-making systems, and hold them personally accountable for the results produced. Where managers express the need for more security, there seems to be a strong ethos of individual performance supported by the necessary management processes, with somewhat less attention given to providing broader goals as a context for individual performance. More important, the performance orientation factor is rated a great deal higher than compensation and also somewhat higher than human resource development. One of the reasons managers in these organizations indicate a desire for more security may be that they find the actual and potential rewards to be inconsistent with the demands being placed upon them.

Where security is greater than desired, overall climate ratings across all factors are lower, a finding that in itself conveys lower morale. The profile of this type of organization is in direct contrast to that in which security is too low, in that the demands placed upon people (performance orientation) are viewed as lower than the potential financial and personal rewards (compensation and human resource development). Both individual and organizational performance planning are quite weak, suggesting that the demands that the organization placed on itself and its people are not high. This finding may be saying in effect that too much attention is being paid to individuals and their financial needs relative to the organization's needs to establish and enforce standards of performance. In the more extreme cases, people may be saying that they feel the company overpays in light of what it expects from most of its managers.

Perceived imbalances between ratings of security as it exists and security as managers feel it should exist may have their roots in imbalances elsewhere in the organizational climate. Looked at from this perspective, the data suggest that an organization might consider changes in its climate that will enhance its ability to attract, retain, and motivate the type of manager it presently employs. Alternatively, the climate may be appropriate, and the organization should attract different types of people, individuals who are most motivated by the existing climate.

Organization Size

Participating organizations in our climate survey have ranged in size from fewer than 1,000 to more than 100,000 employees. In this broad size range, the crucial characteristic to emerge is the tendency toward more formality in the management processes of the larger organizations. Managers in the large companies, when compared to those in the smaller ones, indicate that overall communication is better; organizational goals are clearer, and planning to meet goals is more formal and complete; and individuals are clearer about the results expected of them, and the measures to gauge their performance are better defined.

These trends are corroborated by an entirely different type of survey distributed among personnel officers.[6] Data on the personnel activities in more than 800 U.S. organizations indicated that larger organizations tend to issue more written communication covering more topics. Also, communication tends to become the formal responsibility of a communication department in these organizations. Larger organizations were more likely to adopt formal performance planning systems, such as management by objectives, which, by their very nature, should foster clarity of performance expectations and performance measures.

The size of an organization seems to have no effect on some other climate elements, including the vitality of the organization, its management style, and its compensation system. Large organizations evidently can, in the view of their managers, be every bit as dynamic and responsive and offer as much individual responsibility as smaller organizations. Of course, this finding does not take into account the number and geographical dispersion of locations or the nature of the organizational structure, all of which may intervene in the manager's own concept of size and the ability of the organization to respond and to delegate in a particular manner.

Capital Intensity

The needs of highly capital-intensive businesses may foster a different style of decision-making from those in which physical plant and equipment investment is a smaller part of total assets. The decision to invest in new plant and equipment is rarely that of one individual in an organization. Consequently, where these decisions are frequent and the dollar amounts being considered are large, a greater degree of information, review, and group decision-making is found.

Contrasting climate results of highly capital-intensive industries, such as utilities, heavy manufacturing, and mining, with less capital-intensive manufacturers as well as retail, technical services, financial services, and others supports this concept. Managers in capital-intensive industries see the decision-making process as slow, but based on a great deal of information. These organizations also have more limited patterns of delegation. In contrast, the more people-intensive organizations tend to allow greater delegation of authority and are viewed as more venturesome and innovative in style.

Stages of Business Development

Just as climate goals vary with organizational differences, they must also be adjusted to the organization's stage of business. Of course, the stage of business often applies to the situation of an entire industry and can be seen to account for the particular climate characteristics of that industry. However, companies within an established field can have individual patterns of development. Whether for an industry or a single company, climate and the business stages are integrally related.

Four stages of business development exist:

1. Emergence—a stage with excellent long-term growth and profitability potentials.
2. Developmental—a stage characterized by high market growth and significant capital requirements for expansion, during which the business usually becomes profitable.
3. Commercial—the maturing phase in which profitability should be good to excellent, while risk and growth are reduced.
4. Mature—the phase in which the growth rate either becomes flat or turns negative and in which profitability has peaked and margins begin to erode.

The business assessment matrix (figure 8-10) provides a set of guidelines for positioning a company or business units of a company within a stage of development. This positioning has several general implications for strategic planning and for the climate picture appropriate for such activities. For example, emerging or developmental businesses that are highly profitable may be trading larger future earnings for current earnings. For commercial or liquidation-phase businesses that have low or marginal levels of profitability, the cost of significantly improving profitability is probably prohibitive, and such businesses might better be phased out.

Based upon their position in the matrix, businesses might develop different strategies, such as:

Pump Prime—large investments in engineering, marketing, plant capacity, and so forth, to establish a position of leadership

Catch-Up—selective investments in the areas where the company is weak relative to competition

	Emerging	Developmental	Mature	Liquidation
Growth Potential	Extremely High	High	Average for All Businesses	None
Industry Structure				
- Size Tendency	Small	Small to Medium	Large	Large
- Number of Firms and Trend	Small but Increasing Rapidly	Many but Mergers and Casualties Occurring	Moderate and Stable	Moderate and Declining
Product-Market Characteristics				
- Price Structure	Low Price Elasticity	Some Price Elasticity	High Price Elasticity	Very High Price Elasticity
- Demand Structure	Small Homogeneous Customer Base	Expanding Buyer Segments	Highly Segmented Demand	Saturated Demand
- Product Characteristic	Highly Differentiated	Moderately Differentiated	Limited Differentiated	Commodity
Financial Characteristics				
- Typical Profitability	Negative to Low	Low to Moderate	Moderate to High	Declining
- Cash Generating Capability	None	Modest	Excellent	Declining
Technological Availability	Limited Possession of Proprietary Know-How	Expanding Base	Public Knowledge	Practical Know-How

Figure 8-10. Business Assessment Matrix

Sustain—continuation of present practices with only fine tuning for maximum efficiency of operation; limited investment required

Turnaround—major changes in products, technology, distribution, and other aspects, to correct a poor position in the industry

Divest—possible selling of a business to a company that is in a better position to capitalize upon its strengths, which the present company cannot do because of limited investment resources or a major deficiency in an area such as raw materials or distribution network.

Because each stage of development on the business assessment matrix and each of these five strategies can most likely be carried out through a different managerial style, an assessment of organizational opportunities and constraints is also necessary in the formulation of a company's goals. Its organizational situation—structure, people, and processes as reflected by its climate—determines its capacity to implement effectively the chosen strategy. Mismatches between strategy and the company's ability to carry it out have led to numerous failures and disappointments.

Although external business risks related to an opportunity are not fully controllable, management can control the internal risks involved with the organization's capability. This capability can be examined through the use of an organization assessment matrix, such as that presented in figure 8-11, which relates the internal organizational characteristics to the four stages of business development. The matrix has been filled in with characteristics that have been hypothesized to be most effective for each stage of business development. Research currently under way is designed to test the validity of some of these hypotheses. Thus, the discussion here is intended to be more suggestive than definitive.

Five major characteristics have been identified on the matrix. The first four describe how well an organization is equipped to make necessary decisions:

1. Delegation—behaviors and procedures that make delegation possible, and the extent and pattern of delegated authority.
2. Decision-making—processes by which decisions are made and communicated; the clarity of decision-makers about goals and limits of authority; and availability, timeliness, and relevance of information.
3. Planning and Control Systems—formal systems for establishing long-range plans and measuring results for control purposes.
4. Responsiveness—the extent to which the people and processes of an organization are able to respond to changing conditions.

	Emerging	Developmental	Mature	Liquidation
Delegation - Freedom to Act - Risk - Innovation	Limited Delegation by Strong Leadership Variety of Schemes are Possible	Highest Degree of Delegation and Freedom Supported	Delegative to Controlled Flexibility in Meeting Fixed Goals	Very Limited Delegation and Freedom
Decision-Making - Information - Clear Goals	Formalized Goals Virtually Non-existent Information Limited	More Information for Decisions General Goals Exist	Information-Based Decisions High Degree of Clarity	Rigid Goals Controlled Information
Planning and Control Systems	Informal, Highly Qualitative (Milestone-Oriented)	Capable of Setting Broad Goals and Measuring Results (Program Oriented)	Supportive of Careful Goal-Setting and Control. (P & L Oriented)	De-emphasize Long-Term Planning Quantitative Controls (Balance Sheet Oriented)
Responsiveness to External Conditions	Limited Responsiveness at First Focus on establishing a Position	Highly Responsive Adapt to Market Opportunities	Less Responsiveness required due to Decreasing Rate of Change in Markets	Responsive but under Very Limited Conditions
Integration and Differentiation	High Degree of Differentiation Integration at Top	Decreasing Differentiation Integrative Function becoming more "Local" to Markets, Products	Continuing Decrease in Differentiation Integration "Local"	Low Differentiation Integration at the Top (Corporate)

Figure 8-11. Organization Assessment Matrix

The fifth characteristic describes the nature of the interaction within an organization:

5. Integration and Differentiation—the degree to which the required functions in an organization differ from one another and require close collaboration.

Use of such a matrix can help management to determine the status of the organization and its effect on performance, the strategic assets and liabilities of the organization, the strategic requirements for an potential of corporate management, and the nature and magnitude of changes required. Obviously, most of the issues involved in the assessment are climate issues. Two choices for action are possible: Either the strategy can be modified to fit the climate, or the climate can be changed to insure success of the appropriate strategy.

Notes

1. Correlation is a measure of relationship between two variables, such as profitability and climate scores. A perfect relationship is represented by a correlation of 1.00, whereas no relationship is reflected by a correlation of .00. Inverse relationships, such as that which would be found between age and expected life span, are represented by negative correlations.
2. F. Herzberg, B. Mausner, R.O. Peterson, and D.F. Capwell, *Job Attitudes: Review of Research and Opinion* (Pittsburgh: Psychological Service of Pittsburgh, 1957).
3. These items were: "How would you rate this company as a place to work?" and "To what extent are managers within this organization expected to meet demands for high levels of performance?"
4. James W. Gouthro, Francois Quinson, and Arnold Silverman, "Today's Management Climate: Cloudy and Changing," *Electric Perspectives*, 3 (1976):10.
5. George G. Gordon and Bonnie E. Goldberg, "Is There a Climate for Success?" *Management Review*, May 1977, pp. 42-43.
6. "Survey of Human Resource Practices" (Philadelphia: Hay Associates, 1975), pp. 46-50.

Part III
Managing Climate

Strategy and Planning

Business strategy and planning involves the formulation of actions by which an organization attempts to take advantage of new opportunities in its field of enterprise or to correct problems it faces. Climate analysis can be integral to strategy development by determining whether the company's organizational structure, human resources, and management processes are consonant with its strategic purposes.

Typically, the analysis emphasizes those specific functions, such as marketing, that are related most directly to new opportunities, those procedures that explore and prepare for new ventures, and those aspects of human resource utilization that are necessary for strategic success. In addition to measuring organizational strengths and weaknesses in those areas, climate analysis can result in suggestions for improvement which in themselves may develop into fundamental components of the business strategy.

The four case studies to be discussed in this chapter represent variations of the application of climate analysis to strategy and planning. The first case, Cargo Shipping, involves a new president who is attempting to bring a sophisticated management approach to a firm that has been primarily entrepreneurial in character. The second, Equipment Manufacturing, represents a more mature organization which is focused too strongly on meeting its day-to-day problems, to the detriment of long-range strategic activities. Thermal Gas is a utility which faces long-term limitations on growth and is attempting to develop strategies and plans to cope with these limitations. Finally, Magnum Foods is a company that wishes to implement a specific change in marketing strategy, but faces severe internal problems in doing so. Together, these cases exhibit a variety of the climate issues that companies face in the area of strategy and planning.

Redirecting Management Processes—Cargo Shipping Company

Cargo Shipping Company is engaged in the transportation of cargo between ports in the United States. Its operations are confined to certain specialty cargoes and specific ports. Under family leadership, the company has grown from a very small operation to one that is grossing hundreds of millions of dollars in revenues each year.

However, two factors have combined to limit potential growth. The first is the restricted opportunities for further growth in its present product and geographical mix. Second, the size of the business has outstripped the company's management processes. As is common in such cases, many decisions are still being made as if the company operates only one or two vessels, although it now has dozens. Furthermore, the company now has the opportunities to utilize much more complex and integrated operations to take advantage of market conditions, but is failing to capitalize upon them. To help Cargo Shipping to meet these challenges, a president was brought in from the outside. This new individual was chosen for his sophisticated managerial skills, which would enable him to build upon the previous entrepreneurial orientation of the company.

The climate analysis was conducted as part of an effort to develop a comprehensive strategy for the company. In particular, it covered people's awareness of the problems of the company and their motivation to make significant changes in its operation. In addition to the standard eight dimensions, the survey included especially designed items on the information basis for marketing planning, market reliability, and marketing vitality. The survey was administered to twenty-seven people in the most significant management positions.

Overall results reveal a set of evaluative conclusions about the company. Its strengths include its role as a pace-setting organization in its field and its venturesome management group, which is receptive to change, desires involvement and responsibility, and is encouraged to be innovative and independent. However, the company's weaknesses tend to undermine this positive potential. Despite the willingness of management, not enough effort is put into new ventures or new accounts. Clear goals and future directions are absent, communications are poor, and personal accountability and performance measures are unclear.

Supplementary items for the Cargo Shipping Company reveal a positive feeling about the company and a great desire for involvement among managers, but an inability to act upon these feelings because of poor communications. Managers do not have the information they need to be aware of happenings in other parts of the organization and they feel especially poorly informed about the strategic direction of the company. They call for more sophisticated information management, in particular a computer-based information system to serve operational and marketing needs. These managers, with positive feelings about their company, are optimistic about the possibility for improvement within the next year; most had already observed positive changes in the management environment in recent months.

Supplementary climate items dealt particularly with the marketing function. Since no data base is available for them, they are presented as averages on a five- or seven-point scale. Inquiry into the information basis for marketing planning (figure 9-1) revealed that managers feel moderately well informed about their customers, but not a step ahead of them in anticipating needs. Furthermore,

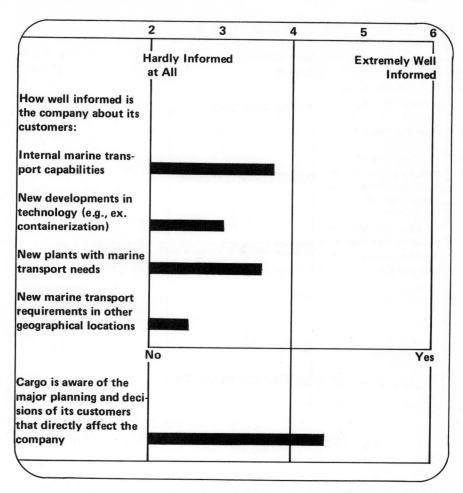

Figure 9-1. Cargo Shipping Company—Information Basis for Marketing Planning

there is little awareness of market possibilities outside the geographical areas already served. Questions related to marketing vitality (figure 9-2) produced a broader range of results. While managers are eager to pursue new business ventures, the company is making only a limited effort to secure new markets and accounts. Greater emphasis should be placed on seizing favorable opportunities while Cargo Shipping still remains committed to existing customers.

Another scale, on which respondents were asked to select those characteristics of the work environment most important to them, measured group motivational patterns.[1] A total score indicates the degree to which a person is

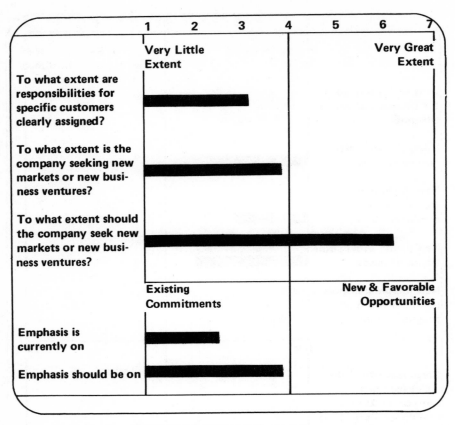

Figure 9-2. Cargo Shipping Company—Marketing Vitality

security- or risk-oriented: Those scoring high on this measure tend to be more risk-oriented and are apt to respond well to increased responsibility, while low scorers are more inclined toward job security, are less likely to take risks, and are more likely to resist change, especially when that change focuses greater responsibility upon them. While 52 percent of the total Cargo Shipping group scored in the achievement-oriented range, 63 percent of those responsible for major investment and marketing decisions scored similarly. Thus, the people who have major roles in developing new approaches to the way in which the company conducts its business display motivation patterns that would support such change.

The climate survey of the Cargo Shipping Company provided important insights into the organization's existing capacity for undertaking strategic planning and implementing changes in its mode of operation. In this case, the climate survey pointed up areas that require corrective action and gave impetus to a change in market philosophy. Most important, however, it indicated that the key people were in tune with the president's own view of the problems facing the company, and were motivated to make the needed changes.

Capability for Goal-Setting and Strategic Planning—Equipment Manufacturing Company

The impetus for this study was the desire of Equipment Manufacturing's top management to obtain an objective picture of the attitudes of its managers toward management structures and processes that would allow the organization to adapt to change and meet its business objectives. A billion-dollar division of a major U.S. manufacturer, the company faced a highly competitive market in which a steady flow of new and improved models was necessary to maintain market share. While the company was not facing any unusual crisis, the ability to bring about purposeful change was critical to its success.

Questionnaires were answered by 276 people at significant managerial levels. The information was compared among functional areas: staff, manufacturing, marketing, finance, engineering, and systems.

The overall impression derived from the survey was that the organization is changing and has managers who are willing to support the change. However, there are strong feelings that top management is very conservative in its approach to the business. This perception, coupled with a strong feeling of urgency communicated from above, left many people confused about the performance standards used to guide responsiveness to change.

Top management (department VPs) views Equipment Manufacturing much more optimistically than do any of the lower level managers. Top management's hopes for the future are important, because this group possesses the principal power to shape that future. However, the failure of lower management to share this enthusiasm needs attention, because unidentified inner troubles can prevent realization of goals.

The managers in the various units perceive highly centralized decision-making which offers little encouragement or opportunity for individuals to use their own initiative in dealing with their business problems. This situation has lead to rigid lines of communication and a severe lack of integration of unit activities. The planning and decision-making processes are seen to have significant weaknesses. The company is judged to be failing to realize the full potential of its employees.

So far the issues covered in the climate analysis of the Equipment Manufacturing Company are generally similar to those of the Cargo Shipping Company. However, while the first survey did not go beyond examining the backgrounds of strategic planning, this one sought specific information about the processes of planning, decision-making, and strategy effectiveness.

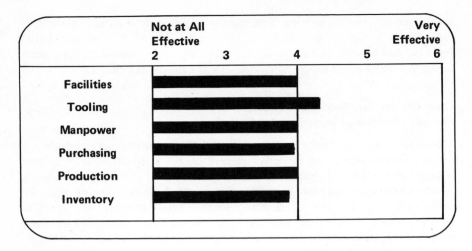

N = 276

Figure 9-3. Equipment Manufacturing Company—Extent of Planning Effectiveness by Area

As shown in figure 9-3, planning is viewed as less than effective in all areas. Interdepartmental differences are not shown because they are slight. The principal concern for management is to identify what elements of the planning process led to this unenthusiastic response.

One source is the typical time span of planning activities. As table 9-1 clearly shows, greater emphasis on long-term planning is desired throughout the company. Managers in the departments feel that they are spending too much time planning for the coming week or month at the expense of the year ahead or

Table 9-1
Percent of Time Spent in Short-, Medium-, or Long-Term Planning: Equipment Manufacturing Company

Planning	Total	Top Mgmt.	Mfg.	Finance	Mktg./ Field	Mktg./ Home Office	Engineering
Short-term (1 wk − 1 mo)							
As is	47.0	20	51	56	59	45	26
Should be	32.2	17	32	44	42	30	19
Medium-term (3 − 6 mos)							
As is	28.2	28	30	29	26	28	25
Should be	31.2	18	37	30	32	29	23
Long-term (1 − 2+ yrs)							
As is	23.9	50	19	15	13	27	47
Should be	35.4	62	31	27	22	41	56

beyond. In fact, manufacturing, field marketing, and finance are devoting more than half of their planning time to the short term. Even top management gives most of its attention to the next six months. The absence of long-range, market-sensitive planning significantly hinders opportunities for expanding into new industrial and consumer markets.

Another possible reason for the ineffective planning is the nature of accounting systems information available to management. Figure 9-4 describes management's reactions to the company's accounting systems. Two main findings emerge: Planning information contains high and low points, and the operating departments are consistently less positive about the accounting systems information they receive than are either staff or finance management. The managers from manufacturing, marketing, and engineering express particular concern about the historical rather than the predictive nature of that information. In fact, all management, except for the finance people, who generated the information, agrees that this is the primary deficiency of that information. In addition, operating department managers, particularly from the marketing field staff, find the information too hard to obtain and poor in identifying and evaluating planning options.

Top management may be more optimistic about the accounting information because it receives more complete information. If sufficient information does

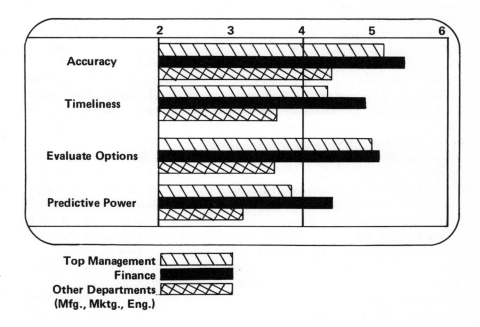

Figure 9-4. Equipment Manufacturing Company—Quality of Accounting Systems Information

exist, the questions then are whether more should flow down into the departments and whether it can provide more guidance for future possibilities, rather than just recording past events.

Because decision-making and planning go hand in hand, it is not surprising that reactions to the decision-making process mirror those to planning. Decisions are seen as reactive rather than anticipatory, delayed and conservative rather than innovative. Furthermore, most managers see decision-making as overly centralized and made at inappropriate levels.

Thus, the planning and decision-making processes, as viewed by most Equipment Manufacturing managers, constrain planning too much in the immediate present and limit planning decisions too much to top management. With this situation, the problem of integration below the top seems all the more plausible. The consequences of such planning and decision-making can affect the basic goals and business strategies of the organization.

Data are also collected on product-line objectives and operation of product committees, the principal vehicle for arriving at product-line decisions. While these data are too lengthy to present here, some of the highlights are worth citing. Light equipment and consumer product lines are viewed as less broad or complete than heavy equipment products, a view held in all departments and at all levels of management. Management generally called for some de-emphasis on an overly broad product line in heavy equipment and an increased emphasis on growing markets in light equipment and consumer products—that is, for a more balanced product mix.

If the new emphasis is to be on greater marketing of existing products, the advanced nature and high quality of these products are two notable advantages. However, if new products are to be developed or if current products are to be exploited maximally, current planning and decision-making processes need to be reexamined. As perceived, product committees are performing no more than adequately. They lack flexibility, decisiveness, and openness to outside ideas. As they are currently composed, the influence of marketing, engineering, manufacturing, and finance is generally seen to be in proper balance. Marketing is seen as having slightly more influence than engineering, which in turn is more influential than manufacturing and finance.

In the departments, particularly marketing and engineering, conflicts emerge over who does and who should have the most influence. Marketing managers feel that engineering has slightly more influence than marketing, but that marketing should have far and away the most influence. Conversely, engineering managers feel that marketing already has a great deal more influence than anyone else, but that a proper distribution would find engineering and marketing sharing the most influential role. These disputes over influence could be one reason why the decisiveness, openness, and flexibility of the product committees have been questioned. Perhaps more guidance from top management about roles and integration of effort in the committee is necessary.

Despite these problems, management sees appropriate directions of change taking place, which are having a positive effect on the perceived climate in the company. For example, people perceive much more coordination among units and regard themselves as having greater responsibility and authority than previously. While these changes appear to be in the right direction, the company's greatest internal challenge will be to increase the ability of people to have an impact upon implementing the company's new efforts. Major management efforts are needed in the areas of intermediate and long-range planning, the development and dissemination of management information, and the integration of the functional units toward corporate objectives.

Strategy Recommendations—Thermal Gas Company

Unlike the climate studies of Cargo Shipping and Equipment Manufacturing, that of the Thermal Gas Company, a utility, uses climate findings to construct a series of specific strategy steps and a procedure for their implementation.

Management climate conclusions revealed serious concerns about the organizational clarity and decision-making structures among the vice presidents and the managerial level reporting to them. Managers find goals unclear and useless as a context for everyday functioning, and planning ill-defined and only short-term. For them, the current structure hinders implementation of strategies and achievement of goals because it fails to provide needed information and frustrates coordination of efforts.

A sense of limited encouragement of individual initiative pervades the organization. People do not feel encouraged to innovate, take independent actions, or take reasonable risks to carry out their responsibilities and increase the organization's effectiveness. The majority of people feel that individual initiative is constrained primarily by internal influences such as organizational structure and management style, rather than by external factors such as government regulations and the availability of natural gas and capital.

While managers accept the need to operate the business more efficiently and economically and toward that end are willing to reallocate human resources throughout the organization, they do not perceive very much unrealized opportunity to reduce costs so as to increase return on investment (figure 9-5). Another problem is that they hold an unfounded belief that major opportunities exist for the acquisition of new gas supplies, which could change future growth prospects. Rectification of this misconception, which leads to a suspicion that unnecessary constraints are being imposed on freedom and innovation, might help establish a more realistic and positive climate.

In addition to these organizational factors, strategic information about the nature of the utilities industry was compiled to provide a basis for planning.

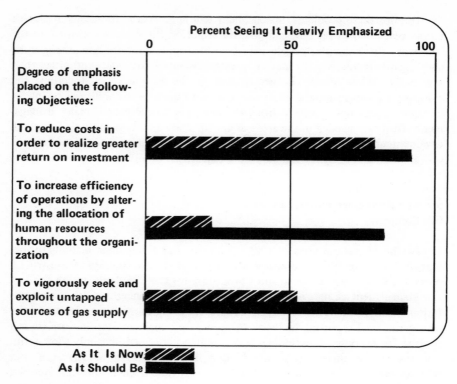

Figure 9-5. Thermal Gas Company—Actual and Desired Emphasis on Various Business Objectives

Because of long-term restrictions on gas supplies and increasingly stringent regulatory action on rates, Thermal will function in the mature stage of business for the foreseeable future.

Changing regulatory practices have altered the requirements for success for the gas distribution business. Gas procurement requires greater effort and skill in the marketplace. Meeting engineering standards requires a narrower range of skills but greater attention to compliance and administration. Increased focus must be placed on operations to assure efficiency and economy. Because growth opportunities are so limited, a marketing capability is no longer necessary.

Because of these circumstances, the mission of Thermal's basic distribution business should be to become a positive cash-flow producer. Within this strategy, it is important to evaluate divestiture, "swap," and acquisition opportunities to upgrade and consolidate properties geographically. Given this mission, objectives must be spelled out clearly in order to

1. Determine a measured approach to meeting engineering requirements.
2. Enable rates to be set in support of longer-term objectives.
3. Determine how appliance sales will be supported within the mission.
4. Determine a measured approach to service that will, for example, support future nondistribution requirements.
5. Determine what accounting changes appropriate to rate-making will support long-term goals.

The company must also focus on growth possibilities beyond the distribution business by evaluating distribution-related acquisitions and nondistribution acquisitions or start-up possibilities, an area of opportunity that the climate data show to have the most promise.

Adoption of such a mission would have organizational consequences. As a cash generator, the company should be run as efficiently and economically as possible, with clear delegation, understanding, and focus. Centers of expertise in rate-making, supply procurement, and engineering should be created to respond to the specific needs of the marketplace. In addition, a top-level position such as vice president of development should be considered, to give diversification and expansion efforts the proper amount of attention and emphasis.

To realize this new organizational structure, Thermal must change from a structure and style more consistent with the needs of a developmental business to one more appropriate to an operation in the mature phase. Currently, managers have a higher degree of autonomy, with freedom to be more entrepreneurial and risk-taking, than business conditions warrant. Yet, the climate data indicate general feelings that initiative is constrained, suggesting that management has not come to grips with the changing requirements. Generally, given the tasks of running a mature business, a managerial overcapacity exists at all levels of the organization, a situation that the climate data indicate is widely understood.

Some managerial characteristics have hindered the strategic direction the business must take. Because of concentration on running the base business and because of failure to develop the many diversification ideas, management has not been responsive on a large scale to changes in the distribution business and therefore has not pursued opportunities to diversify. The capability of managers at the division and district levels is in question. Their limitations could hinder consolidation or enlargement of divisions and their ability to conduct additional businesses.

Because of Thermal's status as a mature business, a serious concern exists about the future vitality of the company. People do not want to be part of a "caretaker" organization. Those at the lower levels worry about development opportunities in a no-growth business, and those at upper levels struggle to maintain the content of jobs that challenged them in the past. To combat this situation, a conscious effort must be made to plan, within the constraints of the business, careers for managers whose skills and experiences are valued and transferable.

Recommendations for change in Thermal Gas covered issues of organizational structure, management processes, and business development. Fundamentally, these changes involved the establishment of a more efficient structure for managing the basic business while placing aggressive focus upon new business development. In each of these areas, the climate data pointed to change that would be both productive for the organization and acceptable to a large majority of management. In addition, certain areas in which management perceptions and situational realities were in conflict were identified. Thus, top management could focus its communications on eliminating the misperceptions and implementing the needed changes.

Marketing Strategy—Magnum Foods

Unlike the climate analysis conducted for the Cargo Shipping Company, which had a general concern for management's ability to take advantage of new marketing opportunities, the study carried out for Magnum Foods, a processor and distributor of agricultural products, sought information to be used in taking the specific steps needed to achieve three key marketing objectives:

1. To increase sales by improvements in sales through dealers and direct sales to large accounts, placing primary emphasis on switching from a heavy dealer-sales orientation to a more balanced mix of dealer and direct sales.
2. To establish a higher degree of experience and stability in the sales force by reducing turnover.
3. To sell a premium product at premium prices.

Although the three objectives are interrelated in that the move to direct sales would place different demands upon the sales force and must take into account both prices and product, increasing direct sales took top priority for Magnum.

However, the climate data revealed that existing attitudes among sales managers present major barriers to the implementation of a marketing strategy focused on direct selling. In fact, as indicated in figure 9-6, 86 percent of division sales managers and 69 percent of district sales representatives prefer to focus business development on dealers.

The sales force feels that its success remains with the dealer and that departure from dealer sales means risking current business, risking failure, and getting little reward for the effort. The high personnel turnover in sales at Magnum compounds the problem in two ways. With an average 29 percent turnover during the past three years (72 percent of which is voluntary), the uncertainty feared from a major shift in sales strategy could produce an even

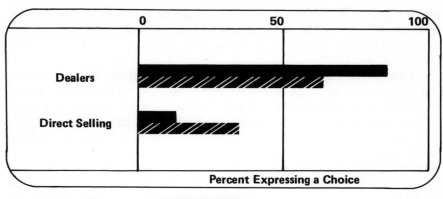

Division Sales Managers (12) ████████
District Sales Representatives (96) ▨▨▨▨

Figure 9-6. Magnum Foods—Preferred Focus of Business Development Efforts

higher turnover rate. Also, the profile of inexperience in the sales force, with 45 percent of salespeople having less than four years' service, adds to the difficulty of implementing a new direction. The inexperienced people cannot provide leadership, and those with experience must devote so much time to covering for the new people that little time is available for growth. Division managers, who should be senior salespeople, are able to devote only 14 percent of their time to cultivating new prospects.

The high-price, high-quality marketing strategy causes additional difficulties because it is counterproductive to sales growth and causes some acceptance of the status quo among the sales force. While 81 percent of the Magnum sales force see the company's products as higher in quality than those of its competitors, only 29 percent see a greater demand for them. Many salespeople feel frustrated by loss of the opportunity to compete on a purely price basis and therefore do not feel encouraged to seek new business. Certainly, many weaker and newer salespeople do not seem capable of selling the "quality" philosophy to new accounts. This situation makes the sales force even more reluctant to consider a major change in marketing direction.

The climate study revealed another significant barrier. While sales management style is considered effective for maintaining existing business, it is not seen as providing leadership to force change to direct sales. Overall style appears to be more gross-results oriented than specific-demands oriented. But even the effectiveness of the gross-results approach is diminished because of division managers' grounding in dealer sales and of inexperienced sales representatives.

While salespeople and sales managers are unusually clear about expected results, they (especially the managers) are less clear about plans to achieve the results (figure 9-7). The overall plan does not appear to be translated adequately into action steps in the field. This may exacerbate the division managers' reluctance to place heavy demands on their personnel, for fear of added turnover.

Although the climate at Magnum Foods might lead one to be pessimistic about its chances of attaining its marketing goals, the company does enjoy a number of significant positive features that could provide a basis for success. Morale, despite compensation problems, remains exceptionally high. Sales personnel see Magnum as "one of the best places to work," and the company scores high above the norms in the areas of encouragement of individual initiative, organizational clarity, organizational integration, and human resource development. The company enjoys overall health. These climate data provided the basis for a series of recommendations aimed at correcting the sales problem at Magnum and allowing the company to achieve its desired change in direction.

To reduce turnover, better prescreening of applicants and management of the training program is needed. Specifically, a program of pre-employment testing is needed to assure that those hired have the necessary personal characteristics and the desire to succeed in the sales job. The time between hiring and promotion to the position of district sales representative should be shortened, and training program benchmarks and salary increases should be used to give trainees a feeling of progress.

The high-price, high-quality strategy requires a more mature salesperson and a more sophisticated approach than usual. Many salespeople and division managers need assistance in selling this strategy. Therefore, additional training should be provided to accelerate the process whereby salespeople feel comfort-

Figure 9-7. Magnum Foods—Clarity of Direction

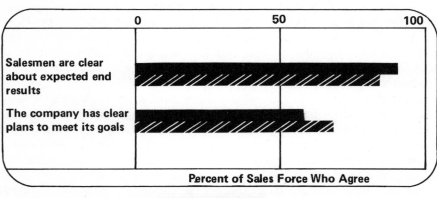

able selling a high-price, high-quality product. Also, proper models should be introduced early in each person's career, by placing trainees in areas where they can see firsthand some examples of successful application of the strategy.

The company's management style must become more directive and demanding to produce the change to direct selling, especially since so much opposition to the goal exists. Division managers and top management should meet to discuss candidly and to reconcile the difference between the current focus on dealers and the direct-account marketing plan. A marketing feasibility plan should be prepared to document more specifically the direct-market opportunities and strategies necessary to achieve sales goals. This plan would not only provide direction in the field, but would also lend credibility to the marketing goal of direct sales.

Without a doubt, Magnum Foods would have had little chance of succeeding if it had attempted to implement its new sales strategy without the direction provided by the climate analysis results. Not only are its personnel opposed to the strategy, but its current management style is inadequate to the task. Although the climate data point to severe problems in implementing the desired changes, they at least allow the company to plan realistically to confront those problems.

Note

1. Ronald J. Grey and George G. Gordon, "Risk-Taking Managers: Who Gets the Top Jobs?" *Management Review*, November 1978, pp. 9-11.

10 Organizational Restructuring

Restructuring to Increase Sales Volume and Profitability—Driver Corporation

In some cases, the problems of a company, whether caused by changes in its external circumstances or by deficiencies in its internal operations, may call for a thorough restructuring of the managerial hierarchy and its relationships. Climate analysis plays an essential role in this process by pinpointing the structural problems and providing information that can serve as the basis for effective change. Such reorganization was required for the Driver Corporation, a producer of original and replacement automobile batteries.

The Driver Corporation is clearly facing severe difficulties. It is losing its usual share of the market and its dealers, its basic product is becoming obsolete, and its own managers rate it as a poor place to work. Extensive corrective measures are necessary to reverse this decline. Since the distribution network represents a major problem area for the company, a study was conducted with the goal of designing an optimal organization for original equipment (OEM) and aftermarket sales.

Delineation of Drivers' problems in the context of those of the entire automobile battery industry revealed several key sources of difficulty.

The transition to maintenance-free batteries with substantially greater longevity has been the primary influence.

The increasing cost of owning and operating an automobile has caused a drop in unit growth from 4 percent to 2 percent, with an attendant impact on the growth of the battery industry.

The net effect of these trends is that industry shipments are predicted to grow only 2 percent over the next five years.

The volume and profitability trends are likely to affect the structure of the marketplace in that low profit levels, coupled with needs for large capital expenditures, may precipitate an industry shakeout.

Because small dealers are going out of business, selling out to larger dealers, or buying up other dealers having greater authority with manufacturers, companies must own significant distribution systems to remain a force in the business.

The market and competitive characteristics place Driver in a declining phase of development. The advent of the maintenance-free battery has complicated the situation by necessitating technological innovations in the product and by reinforcing, if not creating, the declining position of Driver in the industry, because of the company's large commitment to an outmoded design and its late entry into the maintenance-free battery field.

The climate analysis showed Driver's sales and marketing organizational structure to be inappropriate for the current state of the battery industry. While the product line was very narrow, the organization functioned effectively, but with new products broadening the line, the organizational structure itself has become a liability. Its greatest deficiency is the inability to mobilize its resources to go to market quickly and effectively with competitive products. Therefore, a thorough study was made to prepare a systematic plan for restructuring the sales and marketing operation, with special attention to necessary organization, balance of markets and product lines, role and location of support functions, interrelationships of corporate and division functions, need to streamline accountabilities, and need to increase marketing emphasis.

The findings of the organizational study were based on interviews with 76 key Driver personnel at various levels in headquarters and field positions, mostly in sales, but including related areas such as development and advertising; climate data collected from 221 additional personnel in these fields; reviews and analysis of company-supplied data such as sales plans, compensation programs, and research studies; and industry data. Climate results are presented in two formats, for the overall company (figure 10-1) and for four categories of organizational assignment—corporate staff, sales division staff, zone managers, and zone staff (figure 10-2).

The only climate dimension that receives a strong overall rating is performance orientation. On all other dimensions except human resource development, Driver is rated below average, with the lowest scores on management style, organizational vitality, and compensation.

Differences in climate become evident when the total sample is broken down according to the four organizational areas. The corporate staff is most concerned about the company's lack of leadership in the industry and about the reward system. On the positive side, it finds clearly defined goals, good communication and cooperation between groups, accountability for actions, challenging jobs, a matching of people and assignment, and a potential for personal growth within the company.

The sales division staff is the most negative, possibly reflecting both organizational structure and frustrations with its inability to have an impact on sales. These individuals feel that they have no involvement in planning, insufficient information to make decisions, and little freedom to act or innovate. They are discouraged by the lack of organizational responsiveness to change and feel that the organization is a follower, with an inordinate amount of time taken to make conservative decisions.

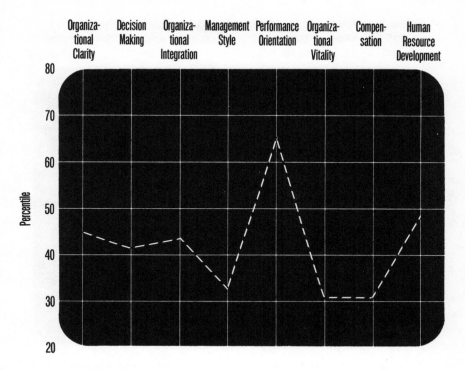

Figure 10-1. Driver Corporation—Overall Company Results

Zone managers are also concerned about the company's role as a follower in the industry and about inhibitions on their freedom to act and innovate. But they are clear about their goals, their ability to manage their operations, and their accountability for achieving goals. The development of people from within the organization and the challenge offered by the jobs are very important to them.

The zone staff people feel limited in their opportunities to act on their own and be innovative, and they voice disapproval of the slowness of the organization to act. Like the zone managers, they feel satisfied with their goals, the challenge of their jobs, and their ability to perform at high levels.

Several special items on the questionnaire were related to Driver's competitive market position and its interaction with its customers. Respondents from all organizational groups agree that customer royalty is low for both the short and the long range. Although the company's prices are seen as at least competitive with its major rivals', the quality of its product is judged as lower than that of these competitors.

In identifying strengths and weaknesses of OEM and aftermarket sales, interesting differences emerge, based on the level of the respondent. Concern for

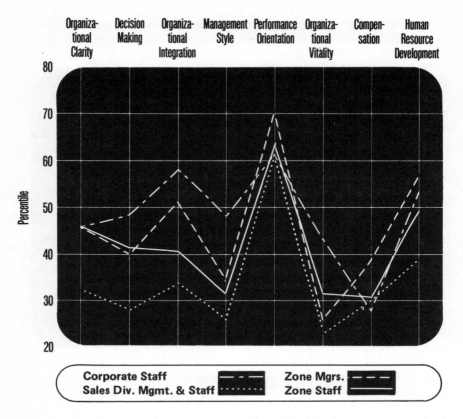

Figure 10-2. Driver Corporation—Unit Results

the product line is a strong issue for lower levels of management, perhaps because they are receiving confusing information as to the product goals of the company. The top management sees the company's financial positions as strong now and in the future, and they see strength in the sales force. However, this group anticipates only modest overall improvements in the development of new products.

In assessing the factors that hinder Driver sales (figure 10-3), all four of the organizational groups specify the inappropriate assignment of authority. Only the corporate staff does not regard excessive formality as a problem, and only the zone staff does not single out the lack of a comprehensive marketing strategy. Both the sales division and the zone staff blame poor channels of communication, but the other two groups do not.

Those surveyed were also asked to rank general strategies according to their potential for enhancing growth in the company's earnings. The development of

	Corp. Staff	Sales Div.	Zone Mgrs.	Zone Staff
Authority Inappropriately Assigned	X	X	X	X
Too Much Formality		X	X	X
Lack Of Comprehensive Marketing Strategy	X	X	X	
Poor Channels Of Communication		X		X

Figure 10-3. Driver Corporation—Major Perceived Factors That Hinder Sales

new products and markets was ranked first in long-term and second in short-term importance. Growth of present operations ranked first for the short-term and second for the long-term. Yet the overall perception of the company is that the introduction of new products to meet market needs is long overdue and that previous performance has not been responsive to the competition.

When these responses are analyzed by organizational group assignment, it becomes evident that sales employees desire growth of present operations more strongly than do other organizational groups. But middle-management groups in the corporate staff stress the development of new products and markets as the most appropriate strategy for growth in earnings.

The great gap between the perceptions of the corporate staff and those of the field organization is very striking, especially in areas such as organizational vitality, problem resolution, and management style. The fact that sales division personnel exhibit the lowest climate level is also disturbing. Many people question the value of the sales division both in the field and in corporate headquarters. People in the division may be demoralized because they have no real role in the organization as it is presently structured. On the basis of the climate survey, the division's contribution to the company's mission must be reviewed.

The key dimensions of concern for change are the management processes and the availability of managerial talent. A revised organizational structure would be fundamental to mobilizing these resources. Without doubt, the present structure is inadequate. The current staff does not appear to be positioned effectively, a fact complicated by the confusion existing over multiple and parallel reporting relationships. The structure is also oriented toward sales rather than development of new products, and staffing is lean at implementation levels.

In terms of overall business strategy, different elements of the company are pulled in various directions. Central management is devoted to volume sales versus profitability; sales division management is preoccupied with retail sales profitability; many corporate-level units are driven by selling batteries as original equipment. Although planning is acknowledged as crucial, it usually focuses on what needs to be done after the decision to act has been made, rather than being an integral part of the decision process. As a result, when new products are introduced, the planning procedure is rarely timely enough to allow maximum exploitation of market events.

The present management process uses an extremely disciplined approach which expects and requires a high level of loyalty. Involving an elaborate system of checks and balances, it has generated multiple decision and approval levels which delay implementation. One of the most distinct characteristics of the process is the inclination to assign accountabilities without the equivalent of freedom to act. At the same time, as an outgrowth of the checks-and-balances system, authority to approve or disapprove has been given, but without clear identification of accountability for results. In addition, the organization appears to suffer from a failure to share market and cost data.

Because the field force does not seem to be trusted, it is required to spend an inordinate amount of time seeking approvals and direction from central management instead of concentrating on the marketplace. Most of what is accomplished occurs because of personal relations with headquarters, not because of accountabilities or a responsive chain of command. Collectively, these issues prevent close alignment of performance measurements, rewards, and the ability to affect sales results.

A final set of critical issues relates to people. Throughout the organization, individuals suffer limited horizons, which leads them to respond almost entirely to current problems instead of to long-term development. Those in OEM sales harbor a considerable distrust of corporate intentions and actions, especially as they apply to personal concerns such as promotions and salaries. The rigid management process combined with a remarkable uniformity of thought has produced a closed culture where mavericks and doubters are not welcome and where the introduction of new blood into the organization is rejected. The process is geared to reproducing itself with similar people.

The climate survey, which offered information on necessary attitudinal changes, and the personal interviews, which helped identify the business, market, and organizational needs, provided the basis for identifying the major objectives and benefits crucial to any recommendations for organizational restructuring. Clearly, the overall negative view revealed by the climate audit established basic evidence for the necessity of change.

The implementation plan for reorganization that emerged from the study and data analysis focused on three basic goals:

1. Redirection and expansion of the company's emphasis from a sales orientation to a coordinated product planning, marketing, and sales orientation.
2. Elimination of a significant contradiction in the present organization—

assigning accountability without authority to act and assigning authority without accountability for results, a situation in which too many people can reject and too few can approve.

3. Alignment of the organizational structure with the product life cycle or phase of market development, thus bringing the structure in line with marketplace realities.

Recommendations for restructuring the Driver Corporation emphasized six points: creating real production management, establishing a new marketing function to include research, advertising, training, and monitoring; strengthening district management; holding each zone accountable for profit margins; balancing sales through all channels; and eliminating regional-level redundancy. To accomplish these points a detailed reorganization plan was drawn up to include restructuring of marketing, product management, OEM sales, aftermarket sales, the zone structure, marketing services, marketing accounting, advertising, private brands, manufacturers' sales, supply and service, and the pricing mechanism.

Consideration of the new place of marketing in the corporate structure is indicative of the nature of the recommended changes. The proposed magnitude of the marketing position is shown in figure 10-4, with "executive vice president—marketing" suggested as the title for the top position. The word *sales* was dropped to emphasize how critical total marketing, a concept neglected in the past at Driver, is to future success.

A basic feature of the proposed structure is a significantly strengthened product management function as separate from aftermarket sales, OEM sales, or private brands. Marketing services has been created as a new function to provide

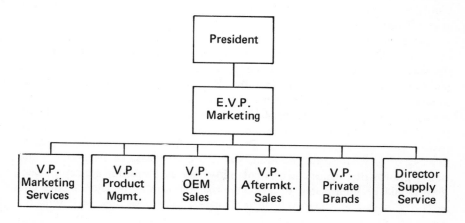

Figure 10-4. Driver Corporation—Proposed Organization of the Marketing Division

a centralized support division for the other functions. Another new and consolidated function, supply and service, was created to pull together those elements that supply merchandise to be sold through the zones.

Obviously, changes of such scope cannot be applied to any organization without a detailed implementation plan and timetable. The first step calls for identification of potential obstacles to provide a realistic framework for developing an overall master plan that gives actions priority in relation to their feasibility, estimated time requirement, and respective interdependence.

Serious organizational and attitudinal obstacles do exist. In spite of the leveling-off of sales and market potential, many people in significant managerial positions demonstrate a surprising lack of perceived need for substantive change and a great reluctance to alter the status quo. Second, while the company has created a very homogenous and loyal organization by bringing people along from their earliest career years to mature positions, it may not have encouraged the acquisition or development of the kind of people needed for several of the new positions. Therefore, Driver may have to look outside for some of the personalities and professional expertise necessary to achieve major functional changes. Because the present company organization, which is built almost entirely for the mature phase of the marketplace, suffers a considerable gap from the needed developmental-phase organization, a significant amount of time—probably two and one half years—will be necessary to effect the changes.

Sections of the implementation schedule are presented in figure 10-5. For instance, approving the long-range direction would take four months, with steps to identify people's strengths and weaknesses, redesign positions, and communicate the climate results and corporate direction, that is, the fact that titles and responsibilities are being changed to reflect a new philosophy of operation. Similar steps and estimated completion times for some of the other actions are also indicated on figure 10-5.

As important as a climate survey was to determining the nature of the organizational restructuring needed, climate improvements are even more vital to the successful completion of the reorganization plan. Such improvements will require a number of necessary actions. For one, a more formalized process should be applied to the assessment of the current and future potential of each manager. In the area of planning, each organizational unit must be provided with timely information based on agreed-upon goals to assure a satisfactory, coordinated marketing and sales effort. The initial system should include a limited number of goals for each position, which can be measured by accurate and timely information. Once the accountabilities for each position are determined, they should be interrelated to guarantee that the flow of decision-making and authority is clearly understood. The change in the measurement criteria for marketing and sales positions will necessitate an update of the compensation system. Finally, a coordinated in-house and outside developmental program will be necessary to fill some shortages of specific skills.

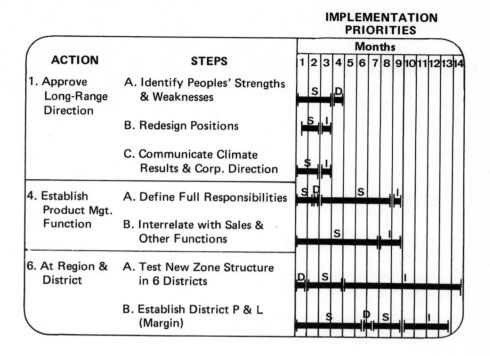

IMPLEMENTATION PRIORITIES

ACTION	STEPS	Months 1 2 3 4 5 6 7 8 9 10 11 12 13 14
1. Approve Long-Range Direction	A. Identify Peoples' Strengths & Weaknesses	S D
	B. Redesign Positions	S I
	C. Communicate Climate Results & Corp. Direction	S I
4. Establish Product Mgt. Function	A. Define Full Responsibilities	S D S I
	B. Interrelate with Sales & Other Functions	S I
6. At Region & District	A. Test New Zone Structure in 6 Districts	D S I
	B. Establish District P & L (Margin)	S D S I

S = Study or Prepare
D = Decide
I = Communicate/Implement

Figure 10-5. Driver Corporation—Sections of the Implementation Plan Chart

While each of these actions is integral to one of the dimensions of climate, the ultimate objective is not to change the climate but to change the business performance. Yet because the study showed that the current organizational structure and management processes encompassed a number of impediments to performance, a change in the management climate will be necessary to improve business results. Thus, a measure of climate can serve as an intermediate criterion of the effectiveness of change. Will the survey participants perceive increased clarity of roles, concentration on marketing performance, and all the other objectives of the current recommendations in a year or two? If not, the changes that were made will have failed to make an appropriate impact on the people involved, and there will be no reason (barring radical changes in the economy) to expect increased business success. If, on the other hand, the company is seen to be managed in a more effective manner, an improvement in the bottom line can only be a matter of time.

Restructuring of a Service
Organization—the Agency

While the Driver Corporation required reorganization because of reduced profits and declining sales, an organization that is not judged by profit and loss may call for restructuring to improve its efficiency, its capabilities, and its use of human resources. The specific case to be discussed involves an actual federal agency with regional offices serving a large number of clients and providing a substantial amount of benefits. Here it will be simply called the Agency. The study was conducted to revise the regional office structure.

The functions of the offices may be divided into seven major areas, four of which are basic to achieving the missions of the Agency and three of which have an impact on its long-range survival, growth, and effectiveness. The activities basic to the missions are

1. Intake—informing clients of available benefits and services, assisting in filing claims, and initiating actions to deliver benefits.
2. Processing—obtaining required information to determine eligibility for benefits and services, evaluating claims, counseling eligibles as to how to use claims, insuring most effective use of services.
3. Output—taking actions to provide benefits and services.
4. Process support—providing administrative, legal, and financial support to the intake, processing, and output functions.

The activities that influence working environment and therefore the long-range situation are

5. Personnel administration—assuring capable and motivated staff for field activities of the Agency.
6. External relations—maintaining supportive attitudes in affected publics for Agency activities.
7. Support services—providing general facility and ancillary assistance for field activity operation.

Because the assignments of the Agency and the technology available to it have undergone rapid development in recent years, the existing organization is no longer adequate to the tasks or the methodology of operation needed. Improved technological capabilities in data access and transfer have created increasing obstacles to performance of the Agency's functions on a fully decentralized basis while still providing services to clients in a timely, economical, and professional manner. A new structure is necessary to provide information sources and a communications network for improved planning and decision-making at the regional and national levels. These changes should allow top management to lead the operating units by providing new ideas, action plans, and review techniques appropriate to the Agency's new challenges.

The major change should be a reduction of the situations in which individual judgment is required. Instead, automatic data processing equipment and computers should be used increasingly for routine data location and calculations. Taking advantage of the new technology in this way would free management at all levels from the current heavy administrative and clerical duties and enable it to devote greater attention to improved performance of those activities that genuinely require human judgment.

The main objective of the reorganizational study was to prepare the regional offices for the future by taking into consideration changes in services provided for and needed by clients, introduction of new processing technology, and federal guidelines for cost-effectiveness and regionalization plans. The recommended structure had to give full consideration to current and future service requirements and operating continuity. The changes had to have the capability of being implemented with regard for efficiency and human sensitivity.

The current regional office organization has evolved over a period of years into a stylized, hierarchical grouping of activities consistent with a people-intensive mode of operations, and is heavily dependent upon manual processing of documents. A full-scale organizational study indicated that except for the largest regional offices, greater efficiency and economy would result by consolidating functions in regional centers designated as line management over the regional offices. Support management functions which could also be centralized include selection of personnel for special training and development, management analysis, and, when technologically appropriate, client information.

Because an integrated organization involves the abilities of people to communicate, comprehend, adapt, and interrelate, climate is especially important for an organization such as the Agency. Management personnel at the regional offices were surveyed on eighty items relevant to general climate, relationships with the central office, division interrelationships, and performance standards and measures.

The survey had two major purposes. The first was to indicate the qualities within the regional climates that may enhance or impede changes in organization and to develop programs that would maximize the ability of the Agency to adapt to changing demands and modes of operation. The second was to identify existing or potential problems that may not have been identified in other aspects of the total organizational study.

The general climate throughout the Agency shows a difference from the average organization only in two dimensions that have a negative trend, organizational clarity and human resource development. The regional office managers feel that their accountabilities, goals, and performance measures are below average and that the Agency lacks sufficient depth in management reserves. When considered by functional division, the climate does not deviate widely from the norm of responses. When considered by regional office, the climate of the large regional offices (New York and Chicago) is viewed as less effective than that of the smaller offices in the dynamic managerial aspects of delegation and innovation and in the procedural aspects of management processes and structure. But these differences do not show up in the degree of integration, performance orientation, or managerial quality. In summary, the overall findings reveal the climate of the Agency to be much like that of other organizations, although the Agency is perceived to have a severe problem of staff development and to need improved definitions of results.

The regional offices vary widely in their estimation of the central office's provision of the support that they feel they need. The two largest offices believe that they are not getting enough support, perhaps because they lack flexibility and innovation and look to the central office for solutions to some of their problems. With regard to channels of information, the central office is seen as keeping the regions informed and for the most part as providing adequate support, although some of the functional divisions disagree. However, the central office is viewed as somewhat unresponsive to ideas from the field, a common problem for a large organization that standardizes many of its procedures for different locations.

Inquiry into division interrelationships considered cooperation among divisions and the connection between geographical location and function. The results found good cooperation and little desire for change in the geographical makeup of the function. It was believed that any geographical dispersion would best be limited to those functions that do not have to interact with others in a regional office, or would have to await technological advances that allow quick communications between the outreach unit and the source of data needed for its operation.

Results on performance standards and measures suggest a great emphasis on measurement and definition of individual activities, but less on overall results. Much of the activity that is measured is not related clearly to the desired results and is therefore not perceived as valid.

The general conclusions of the climate study indicate that managers perceive little in the way of immediate and critical problems within the Agency's regional office organization. The most notable exception is in the area of managerial talent, where people expressed considerable concern over the problem of management succession and present efforts to develop management talent. However, contrary to the opinions of the Agency's managers, the evidence obtained through direct study of its operation points to the need for more centralization at a regional-center level, with considerable upgrading of information-processing capability.

Given the staggering load of hand-processed case files, the large numbers of people employed by the Agency, and horror stories about missing information, late payments, and so forth, it is almost incredible that the bulk of management is not more dissatisfied with how the Agency is run. Certainly there is no lack of public and congressional pressure to solve the problems of the Agency. What the results do make clear is the potential for considerable difficulty in implementing any significant changes. Managers do not see the need for or desirability of either centralizing or decentralizing major functions of the Agency. In light of the anticipated resistance, the best results would be obtained by gradually introducing major organizational changes over time and by involving all levels of management in the process of adapting change to their units so that they will feel some commitment to it.

The reorganization would take place in two phases. The first would consolidate major functions within the regional offices and upgrade job involvement and performance measurement to develop the base for the creation of regional centers. Options to utilize new technology and react to changes in the Agency's mission would be left open. The second long-term phase would grant the regional centers major line responsibility and utilize the new technology to allow for improved cost benefits of services to clients and to facilitate further decentralization of tactical implementation from the central office to the regional centers.

Following the guidelines developed through the climate analysis, a careful program of communication and paced change was developed. In light of the gap between perceptions and reality, the initial phase had to deal with the assumptions and standards under which management was operating. Once these were opened to examination, the process of planning for change with those involved became more feasible. Thus, the climate analysis in this case was more useful for pointing up conflicts between reality and perception than it was in highlighting specific problem areas.

Restructuring for New Product Development—Clerical Equipment Company

It is not unusual today for a company to be overtaken by rapidly advancing technology and to find products that had been successful for decades becoming suddenly obsolete. The Clerical Equipment Company was in such a position when its entire line of mechanical equipment for office functions fell far behind electronic applications which performed the same and more complex operations faster and more efficiently. The new competition was coming mainly from the electronics industry instead of from traditional rivals.

Clerical Equipment had no choice but to phase out its old products and develop an entirely new, electronic line. But technological development was a secondary problem. The real challenge involved the reorientation of management to adapt to the marketing future of the company.

Climate analysis played a vital role in a management organizational program that had three major objectives:

1. To identify those strategies that best anticipate and are responsive to the short- and long-term future.
2. To organize, structure, and integrate the activities crucial to the company's capability for achieving the objectives defined by corporate strategies and market trends.
3. To identify and develop the talent needed to meet the stated objectives at the top corporate level.

The overall study included three primary elements. First, individuals were interviewed to gain an understanding of the functional operations of the company. Second, a climate questionnaire was distributed to all individuals in the top four levels of management. Finally, the key executives met for three days to discuss the findings of the first two steps and to outline preliminary approaches to meet the challenges facing the company. The interviews of the first phase resulted in an understanding of Clerical Equipment's competitive situation in its industry and identified several central issues related to this situation.

Three functional businesses were delineated according to product area: mechanical equipment, dedicated systems, and general-purpose systems. Mechanical office equipment constitutes a business of relatively little complexity. Customers require no special expertise to use the products, and salespeople require no systems knowledge to sell them. Because the market for these products is disappearing, this business needs no particular strategic or organizational emphasis other than that needed for effective liquidation.

Dedicated systems, which are combinations of electronic equipment limited in processing capability to one or a few applications, may be the business of Clerical Equipment's greatest growth opportunity. Marketing such systems requires considerable knowledge of the problem to be solved by the system, the ability to design an appropriate system, the ability to make the system work, and the capacity for training the customer to use the system. Since processing flexibility is not an issue for potential customers, buying decisions are based on relative price, performance, and servicing capability.

General-purpose systems, which are computer-based systems capable of performing a wide variety of applications, lie squarely in a field dominated by the major electronics firms. Although price and performance play important roles in buying decisions, processing capability and flexibility are equally important. The key to competing with the established firms in this area seems to focus on those specific niches where Clerical Equipment's product is superior and to concentrate on upgrading existing systems to the superior products.

Because of these factors and its position within the industry, Clerical Equipment had decided to follow this strategy:

Phasing out mechanical equipment and develop electronic replacements.

Placing major emphasis on developing dedicated systems for selected markets and maintaining technological and marketing superiority in such equipment while devoting substantial resources to upgrading the system's capability of the marketing force.

Giving sufficient emphasis to developing a new upgraded line of general-purpose systems which will enable Clerical Equipment to maintain its current base of customers as well as adding new customers who are moving up to their first system.

The interviews held with key personnel also revealed a number of major organizational needs for accomplishing the strategy. Among these were

Upgrading the financial function from one of scorekeeping to one of prediction, financial planning, and other forward-looking activities.

Upgrading the systems mentality of the sales force.

Upgrading management skills to those required for running a systems-oriented business; increasing emphasis given to market planning and forecasting, systems development, systems management, and strategy development.

Focusing more on developmental efforts, not only being more systematic in choosing new products to develop, but also having a substantive intelligence system that allows updating of market forecasts and competitive moves; assuring that systems meet projected volume and margin targets over their respective life cycles.

Clerical Equipment's key personnel considered their company's main problems to be centered on decision-making processes and talent. The overall results of the climate survey reinforced this general perception.

Although organizational goals are a bit clearer than average, the planning systems leading to accomplishment of these goals are less well defined and complete. Both planning and decision-making are seen to be very short-range, and many decisions are made with insufficient data to support them. Furthermore, while innovative thinking is strongly encouraged, there is very little freedom to act below the vice-presidential level. Thus, even short-term operating decisions flow to the top of the organization. One of the results of this pattern is that the strong sense of integration believed to exist at the upper levels is not supported at the third or fourth levels, where low cooperation and understanding of job interrelationships are found (figure 10-6). Given the need to develop a systems orientation in the business, the current organizational pattern and processes are severely deficient.

There is strong performance orientation characterized by strong challenge and concern for clearly defined and measured results, but satisfaction with the quality of human resources and their development is below average. The company is perceived to be weak in its ability to develop management resources from within, and as a result people believe that there are few individuals ready to move into positions of greater responsibility (figure 10-7). Interestingly, this problem is seen as much more critical by the president than by those below him. Finally, below the vice president, compensation is seen to be noncompetitive and inequitable.

The climate data suggest a number of areas of concern. As Clerical Equipment develops from a single-product organization to one of emphasis on total systems, a high level of integration must be maintained to meet organizational goals. Integration and cooperation are lacking at the third and fourth levels of management. The methods for motivating managers, particularly those at these levels, lack maximum motivational value, and the current management development programs do not appear adequate to support the changes occurring within the organization. Appropriate information systems are needed, along with a long-term orientation to facilitate timely, cost-conscious product development. Such systems are currently very weak.

The climate information, as obtained through both the interviews and the

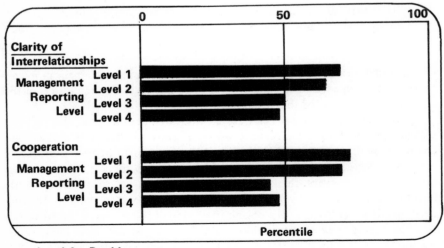

Level 1 = President

Figure 10-6. Clerical Equipment Company—Indicators of Integration Problems

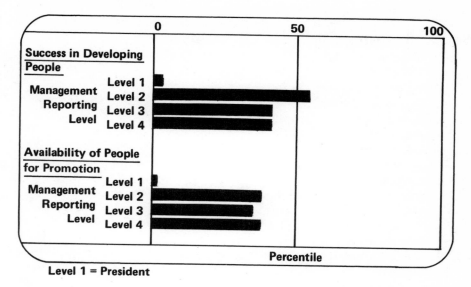

Figure 10-7. Clerical Equipment Company—Problems of Human Resource Management

questionnaires, enabled top management to address the necessary changes in a comprehensive and systematic fashion. Plans for major revision of the management structure, evolving from the exercise, provided for appropriate emphasis on both the dedicated and general systems businesses. Further, changes in management systems for market analysis, forecasting, and planning would allow the company to take a more anticipatory stance rather than merely react to others' moves in the marketplace. Finally, a number of programs were designed to enhance managerial competence and motivation. In this instance, the study forced top management to attend not only to the problems they already perceived in the marketplace, but to the internal climate that had impeded their ability to do so sooner.

11 Rewards and Motivation

The compensation received by an individual for the contribution of his job is much more than a simple material exchange for services rendered. Because it is so tangible, compensation functions as the most immediate and direct commentary on job performance. As a reward it is also a measure of the individual's worth as an employee and, to some extent, as a human being. These considerations place a great psychological burden on an organization's compensation program, which plays a crucial role in developing employee attitudes toward the organization and their relation to it. Compensation in the form of cash or benefits is not, however, the only form of reward an organization offers its members. The opportunity to perform a worthwhile service, personal challenges, feelings of accomplishment, opportunity for growth, and many other factors provide very significant rewards that people obtain from their jobs, and stimulate their motivations to work for a particular company in a particular position. Therefore, since climate and rewards are fundamentally intertwined, climate analysis is vital to the evaluation and formulation of tangible compensation as well as more intangible reward programs.

The following case studies demonstrate the role played by climate analysis in a variety of situations focusing on rewards. The first five address primarily compensation issues, while the sixth is a more general consideration of a motivating climate. For Bluestone Mining, the climate survey was central to an overall evaluation of the company's total compensation and benefits programs, while the Spencer-Huxley study focused on the question of motivation and compensation. Kingsley Insurance Company wished to determine whether its existing climate was appropriate for the establishment of an incentive program. The study for the Kelly-Landor Corporation evaluated attitudes toward the existing benefit program, whereas the survey conducted for the Hazlitt Corporation was used to formulate an incentive plan for a particular category of employee, field sales personnel. Finally, United Diversity applied climate analysis techniques to the problem of motivating high-level staff specialists.

Climate and Overall Management Compensation— Bluestone Mining

The success of a compensation program in any organization can be judged by the degree to which it achieves five basic goals. The program should be

1. Internally equitable, providing for all positions compensation opportunity ranges that fairly reflect the value of each position within the organization relative to all others.
2. Externally competitive, providing for all positions compensation opportunity ranges at dollar levels that the company believes appropriate and can afford and that attract and retain effective employees.
3. Personally motivating, functioning as a vital management of essential results, providing flexibility within a position's salary range to recognize differing degrees of individual performance, and serving to obtain outstanding individual performance rather than simply to reward it when it occurs.
4. Effectively administered, lending itself to maximum decentralization of compensation administration while assuring adequate central control and guidance; possessing a structure that facilitates specific budgeting of compensation increases for any given year, prediction of manpower costs, sound analysis of actual compensation practices throughout the organization, and accurate comparisons of the organization's compensation policy and practice to those of other companies on a timely and ongoing basis.
5. A continuing, orderly, and integral part of the management process which provides for the evaluation of new jobs as they are created and for the reevaluation of existing jobs as changes in content and reporting relationships occur to fulfill future organizational requirements.

Total compensation includes base salary practice, bonus programs, and the various forms of noncash or additional compensation, such as stock options, benefits, and perquisites. In the study that follows, a climate survey played a fundamental role in reviewing the total compensation practice of the Bluestone Mining Corporation. Because the forms and amounts of compensation paid to individuals in a firm should support the style in which the company is managed and the direction that it is taking, the study made a considerable effort to probe not only people's perceptions of their compensation, but also their perceptions of the company and its business environment. These contextual findings have significant implications for climate.

To obtain an overview of the total compensation and benefit programs of Bluestone as they support the motivation of its upper managerial and professional employees, the survey elicited answers to these basic questions about the company's compensation practices:

Are the levels of such practices suitably competitive in comparison with typical practices in American industry today?

Are they designed and administered to assure internal equity of compensation and benefits?

Are the rewards distributed in a visible way which communicates effectively that pay relates to performance, rewards relate to results, and promotions depend upon past and potential future contributions?

Are there gaps that could be filled, with results clearly beneficial to the company as well as to the individual?

Are there unnecessary or undesirable aspects that should be minimized in the future?

The questionnaire findings are based on ninety-three returns, thirty-seven from officers and fifty-six from nonofficers. Where such data were available, results of other management groups on the same issue were compared with those of Bluestone.

The extent to which a company seeks to innovate and change as opposed to following established patterns is one of the most basic issues for compensation, because a highly innovative company usually has to pay at a premium to attract top-quality people. On the other hand, those who run established businesses in established patterns do not command as much. Bluestone presents a paradox in this area. It appears to have been very innovative tactically, in technical advances and the financing of significant operations. Yet from the strategic point of view, the company appears to be highly conservative, reluctant to commit itself to a long-term strategy.

Both officers and nonofficers believe the company to be highly conservative and feel it should be more venturesome. The basically conservative business orientation is reflected in responses to a question that asked to what extent managers are encouraged to take risks in their efforts to increase profits, growth rate, and so on. Most felt discouraged from doing so. Therefore, management risk-taking is clearly not a strongly-held value in Bluestone.

The strategically conservative nature of the company is directly related to the style in which it is managed. In the absence of a clear long-range policy, all decisions that commit the company over any period of time are seen as being made at the very top of the organization. The management style is considered to be highly directive, especially by the officer group. People also feel quite constrained from taking the independent actions necessary for optimum performance of their jobs.

One of the effects of a highly centralized, directive management style is that people below the very top of the organization are not utilized very effectively in management roles. This situation has implications both for development of employees to succeed to top management positions and for how much the organization is presently getting from them. The responses indicate that a lack of opportunity to develop could lead to serious succession problems.

The other side of the difficulty is that people are not seen as working up to their potential. Of course, the degree to which the company demands and expects to get the maximum from each individual has a direct effect upon what its compensation policy should be. Because preliminary interviews with selected executives revealed a belief that the present incentive and stock-option plans does not provide a real incentive, the questionnaire covered topics related to the administration of a true incentive system, such as clarity of roles and measurability of results.

A series of questions about the measures used to judge performance within individual positions brought out many opinions that current measures lack definition, specificity, and relevance. However, most feel that their jobs can be measured reasonably well today and could be measured quite well in the future if appropriate reporting systems were developed. Another finding that appears to be related to the measurability of results is the clarity of the organizational structure. The results here are far lower than those normally found in a company of this size. Many jobs are fractionated, with pieces of the total accountability residing with different people. In a number of cases, individuals report to different superiors for the different functions they fulfill.

The climate results thus far present Bluestone as a conservative company without an expressed strategy or sense of mission. This picture gives rise to the question of whether any real individual incentive compensation program for managers is appropriate when the sense of where the corporation wants to go is lacking in the majority of its executives. Further, the organization functions in such a way that it is difficult to hold individuals accountable for total business results, which are difficult to identify clearly. This set of circumstances makes an individual incentive program even less desirable, since such a program should rest on a firm measurement foundation to be effective.

The climate survey also dealt with attitudes toward Bluestone's compensation program. The reasonable degree of satisfaction with compensation in all groups (figure 11-1) is not surprising in light of external comparisons which show the company to be a high-paying one, even though there is a decided tendency to think that other companies pay considerably better. People may feel overpaid because they see their responsibilities as quite constrained. On the other hand, since communications are regarded as very poor, respondents are also reflecting a lack of knowledge of the company's competitive posture.

Salary administration in Bluestone is viewed quite negatively. Both officers and nonofficers feel that it tends to be subjective, inequitable, and only vaguely related to job performance. They do not have a reasonable understanding of how the program works, and feel that these matters have been communicated very poorly. Even those who have a role in determining salary increases do not feel clear about the provisions and conditions of administration of base salary increases, incentive compensation, or stock options.

In terms of specific benefit programs, the savings plan receives by far the most consistently positive reactions. The adequacy of the retirement program is perceived as fairly high. Although disagreement exists according to geographical location over the desirability of future increases in the form of cash benefits, almost all groups are more interested in increases in base salary than in incentives. People think that the incentives that do exist should be based on equal proportions of their own performance and company performance. The noncash compensation programs seem to be fairly well communicated and understood by all groups.

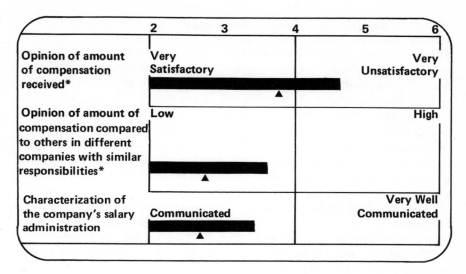

*Average of two items: amount of pay and noncash compensation.
▲Arrows indicate the averages of a limited sample of other companies.

Figure 11-1. Bluestone Mining—Opinions of Compensation and Salary Administration

In summary, executives within Bluestone Mining show overall satisfaction with the amount of their compensation and evidence few problems of a general nature. The area that received most criticism was salary administration and the way in which incentive programs were designed, administered, and communicated.

An important conclusion of the study is that Bluestone does not receive sufficient motivational benefits from its compensation dollars because communication is very limited, with the result that people are quite unrealistic about the competitiveness of their compensation. This situation has three primary causes. The company has no formal job evaluation program to help assure equity in the internal evaluation of jobs; the absence of such a program makes it much more difficult to communicate effectively on subjects such as equity, salary ranges, potential compensation, and competitive position; and the absence also makes it difficult for salary administration to be delegated to any extent, and thus forces salary recommendations to be reviewed and revised at several levels, including the very top, with a resulting poor understanding of cause and effect and of the relation of salary changes to performance. The study also indicates that because of the company's styles of organization and management, it would be difficult to administer any individual incentive program in a way that reinforces managers to act toward predetermined objectives.

The existing incentive program is not succeeding. Managers, even senior managers who have subordinates participating in the program, see little relation between a given reward and that individual's performance. They feel that outstanding performance goes unrecognized or is poorly recognized. At the same time, they feel that the number of participants in the program is so large that many of the awards made are too small to have meaning.

A number of concrete recommendations for improvement of Bluestone's compensation plan, especially steps to develop an incentive plan truly related to performance, emerged from this study. However, to motivate its managers positively, the company's main need is a clear statement of what it wants to be, what its long-range and intermediate objectives are, and how each management job can contribute toward meeting those objectives.

The Bluestone study, particularly because the broad context of climate dimensions played such a key role, demonstrates how climate analysis can be an important element in an evaluation of a company's total compensation and benefit program and of the success of that program in contributing to the company's performance objectives.

Compensation and Motivation—Spencer-Huxley Company

The study of the executive compensation program of the Spencer-Huxley Company, a manufacturer of industrial equipment, used climate analysis to determine the best method for adapting compensation to the individual and group needs, interests, and aspirations of its executive officers. The specific goal was to develop an officer compensation plan that would be an effective managerial process for use in communication, supervision, and motivation.

At the time of the study (in 1972), the company had sales of just under $1 billion, a very healthy growth pattern, and very aggressive plans for the future. Its operations were worldwide and it was organized by profit centers, with considerable input from product managers at the vice presidential level. Because of the nature of the company and its business needs, the plan, along with other management systems and processes, required a design that encouraged innovative and imaginative behavior. Therefore, the climate study concentrated on the motivations and needs of those individuals who were to be affected.

The study revealed that the majority of the fifteen company officers interviewed are highly motivated to fulfill needs for security and belonging and are oriented toward conservation rather than innovation. Such needs will not respond well to compensation programs that lean heavily toward high-risk payouts. However, the requirement of the company is to encourage a higher degree of innovation. Therefore, the compensation program must be designed to satisfy individual security needs sufficiently to allow a shift toward or emphasis on achievement. Correspondingly, allowance must be made for motivating and rewarding those individuals already oriented toward achievement. Spencer-Huxley must also assure proper person-job fit. Those officers oriented toward autonomy and achievement must be placed in positions where they have the opportunity to innovate and contribute, whereas other positions, involving the management of more stable operations, might best be filled by more security-oriented individuals.

A summary of the most pertinent findings of the study are presented schematically in figure 11-2. This display, used as a discussion piece with top management, illustrates the difference between present climate and the desired or optimum climate for both the organization (horizontal axis) and for the personal motivations of the officers (vertical axis) as integrated from climate analysis data, a questionnaire on personal motivations, and in-depth interviews with all senior management.

The findings lead to two fundamental conclusions: The personal moti-

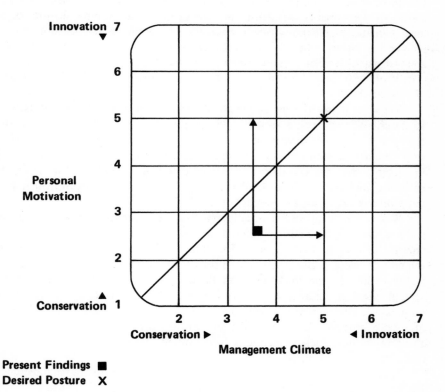

Figure 11-2. Spencer-Huxley—Comparison of Personal Motivation and Management Climate

vations of the officers as a group are currently more conservative than the existing organizational climate, and Spencer-Huxley must develop a more innovative organizational climate to facilitate meeting its strategic plans for growth and profitability. When questioned on their most pressing personal needs as managers, the large majority of officers placed a high value on acceptance and security. Only three of the fifteen stressed achievement. When asked to relate their perception of Spencer-Huxley to their perception of other companies in the field, they found the Spencer-Huxley climate healthy but not very dynamic, vital and profitable but not responsive to changing conditions. Similarly, the company's position in the industry is seen as secure and growing but not very innovative. Responses to questions on decision-making reinforce this picture. The most positive aspect is prudence, with timeliness and rapidity falling behind.

The questionnaire also asked the officers to rate various organizational features as they exist at the company today and as they ideally should be. Clarity of expected results, effective channels for upward communications, and clarity of performance standards are seen as the most desirable features of an ideal climate. Significantly, encouragement of risk-taking and freedom to act receive the lowest rating as ideal climate elements. Those items that show the greatest gaps between present climate and the judged ideal climate are greater clarity of performance standards, of expected results, and of interrelationships of accountabilities.

These responses to general climate questions show a very consistent pattern. In describing the climate as it should be, the officers are looking for greater clarity and structure; they want their jobs defined more explicitly. This result is very understandable in light of the data indicating high needs for security. It is predictable that though these individuals give high priority to the definition of results and performance standards, they do not place an equivalent importance on risk-taking encouragement or freedom to act.

While it may appear contradictory that key managers in a fast-growing company are highly security oriented, an explanation can be found in the actual security offered to these people. The company is known as one that will not tolerate deficient performance, and dismissal of executives in the past has been highly visible. To add to the problem, the pension plan does not provide for any vesting until an individual is fifty-five years old, and then the vesting is progressive. There are stories within the company of executives with many years of service who have been dismissed without any means of retirement. Whether accurate or not, such perceptions have caused company officers to be very cautious in their actions.

It is not surprising that the climate analysis indicates that the company has not been as innovative as its industry might call for. Therefore, the necessary compensation plan must provide for incentives to stimulate innovation while accounting for the basic conservatism of the Spencer-Huxley officers. Before emphasis can be shifted toward achievement, security needs must be satisfied, and those individuals already motivated toward achievement must be provided with appropriate rewards. One of the important recommendations emanating from the study was for a major revision of the pension plan to provide a better base of security.

Further, an incentive plan offering optimal forms of incentive payment was designed, making greater personal security possible to those who have that need and providing more rewards to those already committed to innovative challenges. When an individual can receive an incentive reward in a form that is most satisfying to personal financial and psychological needs, the motivational pull to improve performance is multiplied from that of a fixed-reward plan. Therefore, the recommendation was to provide Spencer-Huxley officers with a wide range of choice as to the manner in which they can receive their payment. In the plan that has been developed, four possibilities are available: cash, company stock, special investment arrangements, or insurance arrangements.

Unlike the Bluestone Mining climate analysis, which related a full climate study to the effects of that organization's compensation program and produced far-ranging conclusions about company goals and planning and management style, the Spencer-Huxley analysis focused on one particular area—a compensation method that would direct the motivations of its executives into behavior more appropriate to corporate requirements. Although the study took heed of the company's objectives and management systems, the major effort was to adapt compensation to the situation as it existed. In Bluestone, compensation problems were merely a symptom of more fundamental problems which required change.

Creating an Incentive Program—Kingsley Insurance

Kingsley Insurance Company is located in the heart of the Sun Belt, and seems to have taken full advantage of growth in that area. Company growth in the past ten years has far outstripped its competition. Kingsley has been very selective in adding new lines, being careful to balance present profitability and future potential.

Climate analysis of Kingsley Insurance was conducted with the specific purposes of determining whether the organization was ready for the implementation of an incentive program and whether such a program could result in significant benefits for the organization. Survey responses were obtained from individuals at management levels: 2 (vice presidents—department heads); 3 (department functional heads); and 4 (all others reporting to level 3).

Judged according to the eight basic dimensions, Kingsley presents a very positive climate picture, with ratings above average on all factors. The company is particularly high in organizational clarity, decision-making, vitality, compensation, and human resource development, and it enjoys a very high level of morale.

With a formal planning system that sets goals that are useful in everyday management, the company appears to have a clear sense of direction which is understood at all levels of management. Decision-making is the highest point of the profile, with a very healthy balance between information gathering and implementation. Vitality is quite high, led by a feeling that the company is extremely responsive to changes in its external environment. Overall, morale within Kingsley is very good and people do not consider the organization to have significant management problems. Where problems do exist, they have great faith that the leaders of the company are taking steps to solve them.

Certain findings are particularly important for the consideration of an incentive program. Positive conditions include timely and innovative decision-making, which leads the company to be a pace-setter in its industry, and the resultant sense of urgency within the management ranks. The existing compensation system is seen to result in very competitive and equitable rewards, with compensation related to performance.

Potential problem areas involve performance orientation and information flow. Personal accountability, performance yardsticks, and performance demands are much higher at the department-head level than at any other place in the organization. Given the clarity of direction and high vitality, it is surprising that people do not feel greater demands or challenges in their jobs. While high tolerance for risk-taking exists at the upper levels, definite blocks appear to hinder upward flow of information, and people feel that they are not encouraged to discuss conflicts.

In addition to the conclusions developed from the standard climate survey, other information relevant to incentives was elicited through certain tailored items. These arose from the premise that an incentive program works best when

The people involved are willing to live with uncertainty in their income if a possibility of higher payment exists.

The organization delegates sufficient freedom to act to individuals so that they can have a significant personal impact upon results.

The measurement of performance is accurate enough so that people find the system credible and are therefore motivated by it.

These questions dealt with job security for management achievement motivation, individual impact on results, performance measurement, performance integration, performance planning, and compensation issues.

The existing level of job security is very high, a type of environment usually not associated with a heavy incentive program. However, those at levels 2 and 3 indicate that less security is appropriate (figure 11-3), an indication that these people have more aggressive motivations than the current climate might imply. Just as significant is a slight shift upward for level 4. These people believe that

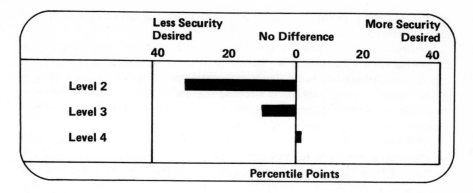

Figure 11-3. Kingsley Insurance Company—Differences Between Existing and Desired Security

the high security offered should be even greater, an attitude that is not supportive of an incentive system.

Similar findings emerged from the series of questions that measured motivation. Sixty percent of the people at both level 2 and level 3 exceed management norms on the need to achieve and willingness to take personal risks to realize this achievement. But while these levels tend to be quite achievement-motivated, only 36 percent at level 4 exceed the norms. Several alternatives exist for dealing with the problem at level 4. The incentive program could be stopped at level 3, including only selected individuals from level 4, or the nature of the program at level 4 could be changed.

While questions on motivation relate to the first basic requirement for an incentive program, those on individual impact on results are relevant to the second. Here, people feel that they have considerable freedom to act, with encouragement to take risks and to innovate somewhat lower but still positive. People at higher levels see much more encouragement to take risks and innovate. Those at all levels feel a high degree of personal accountability for their actions and feel that they have reasonable control over their results. Thus, it appears that sufficient latitude for individual performance exists for the incentive system to have a significant effect upon results.

Responses to questions on the last basic element of incentive, performance measurement, indicate that unit performance is currently measured in a reasonably effective way, with people believing that appropriate new efforts will improve the measurement. Although still positive, measurement of individual performance is seen as less adequate, but also capable of recognizing improvement. Significantly, a good deal of the appropriate measurement is seen to be qualitative rather than quantitative. The standards used to gauge performance are reasonably clear, and people have a strong feeling that they are fair. Once again, this feeling represents a basic faith that upper management does not have unreasonable expectations.

Performance in Kingsley is seen to be heavily dependent upon employees' integrating their efforts; that is, the company's success is viewed as dependent largely upon teamwork, with future success requiring even more such cooperation. Reinforcing this attitude is a feeling that individuals can rely on others in the company to support their work when necessary. However, the reward system is not perceived as encouraging all the needed cooperation.

Performance planning is one method to enhance performance measurement by allowing a company to measure accomplishments against plans that can encompass both quantitative and qualitative objectives. Such performance planning is a useful and reasonably complete management tool at Kingsley. Surprisingly, level 2 sees performance planning as less of a complete process than do either of the other levels, whether referring to performance planning between themselves and their superiors or between themselves and their subordinates. Because level 2 is key to any incentive program, corrective action may be necessary in this area.

Finally, people were asked to give their perceptions of the compensation program as presently administered, to supplement the finding that compensation itself is viewed very positively in terms of equity and competitiveness. Because understanding of the program is only moderate, much room for improvement exists. When questioned on the focus of the compensation system upon long- or short-term objectives, the lower levels regard the focus to be well balanced, with a slight leaning toward the long term. But moving up the management hierarchy, people find the system more oriented to the short term. Such a finding is unusual insofar as top management normally concerns itself with a longer time frame than do lower levels. However, at Kingsley the upper levels see more of a short-range orientation for decision-making. These results probably indicate that people have faith in upper management and therefore assume that its time frame is more encompassing than it actually is. However, it is important to assure that the incentive program will encourage a reasonably long range time frame.

In summary, the climate study supports the conclusion that an incentive program can make a very positive contribution to Kingsley's success. The company's leaders, at least at the top three levels, are primarily achievement-motivated and respond well to incentive opportunity. The company is structured and managed in a way that offers many people the opportunity to have a personal impact upon the company's results. Performance measurement, though it can be improved, is sufficiently credible to support a strong incentive program. Further, the climate study lends guidance to the decisions on how much emphasis should be placed on group versus individual incentive, and on how far down in the company an incentive could produce the desired outcomes.

In the case of the Kingsley Insurance Company, the goals of the climate analysis were narrowly defined and the survey could be constructed to focus on evaluating the company's potential for an incentive program. Interpretation of the standard climate dimensions emphasized those elements most pertinent to incentives. Because the optimum conditions for incentives had been determined by previous experiences, special questions could be formulated to measure the company's fulfillment of these conditions.

Perceptions of Benefits—Kelly-Landor Corporation

A questionnaire prepared for the Kelly-Landor Corporation, a manufacturer of heavy equipment, dealt specifically with issues relevant to the benefits provided to company management. People were asked to indicate the degree to which the various available benefit programs met their needs. Table 11-1 shows the percentage of respondents who indicated that a particular benefit program is not meeting their current needs (the definitions of management levels are generally equivalent to those in Kingsley). Clearly, the bonus plan, stock option plan, and pension plan are viewed quite negatively by large portions of Kelly-Landor managers, and they are the major problem areas of the benefit program.

The current bonus plan (figure 11-4) yields little satisfaction to participants, who see it as unrelated to performance, unfair, of less than average incentive value, and somewhat inferior to plans offered by other organizations. While people are clear as to how dollars are related to points, they find little clarity or fairness in the standards for participation in the plan and do not understand the

Table 11-1
Percentage of Respondents Indicating That Current Benefit Programs Do Not Meet Their Needs: Kelly-Landor Corporation

		Exceptions Noted	
Programs	Percent of Total	Level 2	Level 3
Bonus plan	47		
Stock-option plan	36		
Pension plan	25	31	
Life insurance – after retirement	19	25	25
Long-term disability insurance	17	50	
Life insurance – before retirement	15	46	25
Stock purchase plan	15	31	23
Vacations	11		
Basic medical/health care insurance	9		
Executive physical examinations	9	17	
Moving allowances	7	17	
A.D.&D. insurance – group	6	23	
A.D.&D. insurance – voluntary	4	23	
Excess personal liability insurance	4		
Holidays	4		
Major medical insurance	2		

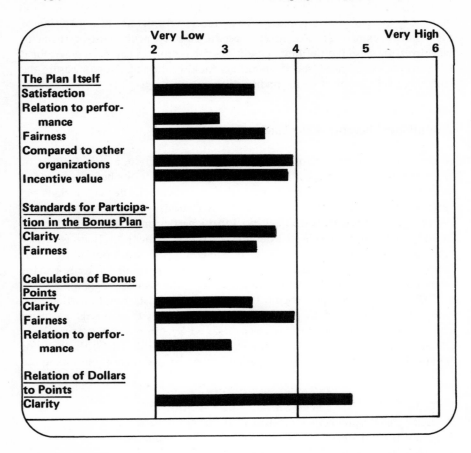

Figure 11-4. Kelly-Landor Corporation—Characterization of the Current Bonus
Plan

calculation of bonus points. They regard these calculations as unfair and
unrelated to performance.

Views of the stock-option plan, while not as negative as those of the bonus
plan, are still on the low side. Respondents feel that the plan is about average as
compared to other organizations and in terms of its incentive value. However, it
is somewhat below average in the amount of satisfaction it provides and in
perceived fairness. Standards for participation in the plan are extremely unclear
and are viewed as being unfair.

To delineate the value of various benefits to Kelly-Landor executives and
managers, information on importance and current adequacy was combined to
yield a perceived "benefit value" index. Data on this index are presented in

figure 11-5, which breaks down the information by reporting levels, since significant differences were found among them. The perceived benefit value analysis considers the degree to which current benefits are seen to need improvement and the degree to which nonexisting benefits are desired, each weighted by their importance to the individual. Thus, the charts in figure 11-5 present both benefits that are currently provided and those that are not. The vertical scale represents their relative value to individuals within the organization, with items of greater importance higher on the chart.

An example may help in reading the charts. If Kelly-Landor wishes to provide a new benefit that is greatly desired, it is clear from the analysis that dental insurance would have strong value, particularly at level 4 and below. Such a benefit, however, would have much less impact on those at higher levels, probably because these individuals do not find dental bills a major source of concern. Instead, they are more interested in travel accident insurance because they do the majority of traveling for the company. The tables make it clear that cash protection and accumulation benefits, such as pension, medical insurance, and bonus, have the highest value for the majority of individuals. The more status-oriented issues, such as country-club or luncheon-club memberships, are quite low relative to other programs.

The findings of this climate analysis of perceptions of benefits were used to develop a variety of specific recommendations concerning improvement of the Kelly-Landor benefit program. At issue here were refinements and improvements, not a single decision as was the case with the Kingsley Insurance Company's possible implementation of an incentive program, which required much more extensive information about management processes. In this case, examination of results by both level and age provided important guidance in designing the most appropriate benefit package for the company.

Sales Incentives—Hazlitt Corporation

Incentive payments have traditionally been used to motivate and reward individuals in sales positions. But because of its special relationship to sales, such a program involves a number of significant considerations beyond those normally applied to management incentive programs.

A study was conducted for the Hazlitt Corporation to develop recommendations for a compensation program for the sales forces in its industrial equipment and mining equipment divisions. The overall goals of this study were to

1. Provide equitable payments to individuals which clearly reflect the relative importance of their contributions to Hazlitt's attainment of revenue, profits, and other marketing goals and strategies.
2. Afford a total compensation opportunity competitive with external pay

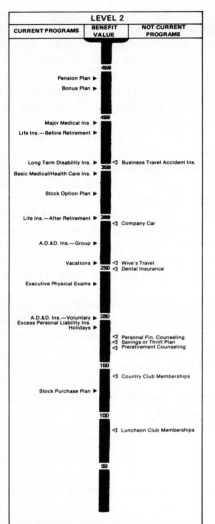

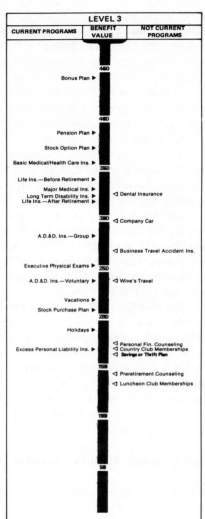

practices, which enables the attraction and retention of capable, qualified sales personnel.

3. Provide high motivation for sustained performance rather than rewarding one-time effort.

4. Create a program that is simple to understand and administer within the company's current practices.

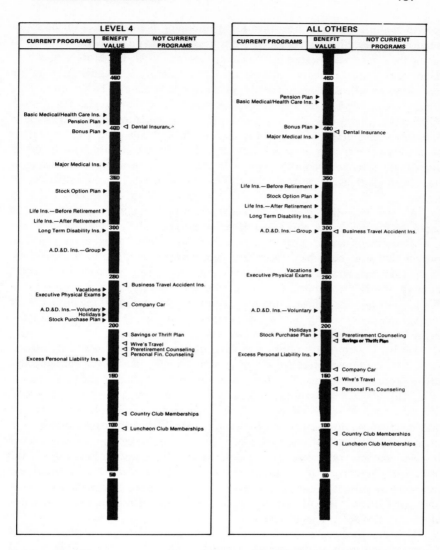

Figure 11-5. Kelly-Landor Corporation—Perceived Benefit Value Analysis

A consideration especially relevant to compensating sales employees is the company's competitive market position according to the four stages of market growth, which are analogous to the stages of business development: introduction and testing, maximum growth acceleration, growth deceleration, and market growth maturity with competition for maintaining market share. In the introduction and testing phase, competition is usually light and forecasts are likely to be highly inaccurate because no experience record exists. Therefore, a high base salary with a discretionary bonus is used to attract a high-caliber staff. In the maximum growth acceleration phase, performance levels may be established for a high commission plan in a market responsive to sales efforts. The growth deceleration phase calls for a more complex compensation plan that involves base salary plus incentive add-on for volume above a sales goal. The foundation of the system is a base salary, which is usually the largest portion of an individual's total compensation award. In this phase, base salary is more modest than in the first phase, and an objective system for making the incentive awards exists.

A sales incentive plan in the market growth maturity phase must be carefully justified on a cost-effective basis. Because of the complexity of the marketing management problems faced in this phase, a managed incentive system that uses both base salary and incentives is appropriate. Incentives are applied to measurable goals which may be expressed in terms of revenue, number of target accounts sold, profit growth, market penetration, and so forth. These goals may be changed quarterly, from year to year, or at the discretion of management, depending on market conditions. In sum, the nature of mature phase businesses requires a more complex goal-setting process.

Hazlitt's competitive position in most markets places the near-term market growth at the growth deceleration or growth maturity phase. As a consequence, the appropriate guidelines for these phases must be applied to the development of a field sales compensation program. To aid in designing the program, a total of 229 individuals were surveyed. Most of these were salespeople, but the group also included service managers, district managers, branch managers, and servicemen. In addition to the eight basic climate dimensions, certain issues pertinent to sales compensation were investigated: the current compensation program, the effects of the current bonus-incentive program, the effort required to achieve incentive awards, preferred compensation mix, preferred commission structure and distribution, view of Hazlitt products and their marketing image, resource allocation, and sales force motivation.

Overall, Hazlitt employees believe the company has reasonably clear organizational goals, above-average encouragement of individual initiative, and an appropriate concern for individual development. However, it is characterized as below average on integration, performance orientation, and management style.

Compensation emerges as a problem area. While the perception of noncash compensation is highly favorable, both salespeople and other employees feel cash compensation is unsatisfactory and not competitive, and fails to meet their individual needs. The current compensation program does not stimulate high levels of motivation because people do not believe that compensation is related to performance and they find little internal equity (figure 11-6).

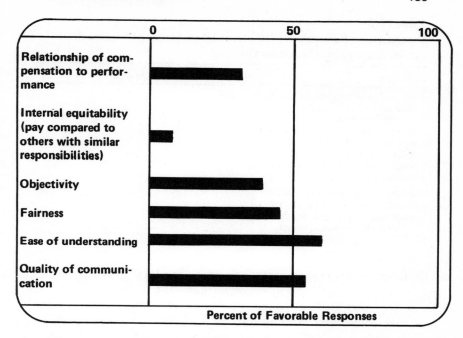

Figure 11-6. Hazlitt Corporation—Current Compensation Program

When questioned on the current bonus incentive program, respondents were evenly divided on whether or not it was effective for encouraging individual initiative, risk-taking, and motivation. One must therefore conclude that the current plan has had limited effect on the performing characteristics it is meant to encourage.

On the whole, the sales force is quite receptive to compensation programs that emphasize incentive awards. The optimal mix preferred by the total sample consists of 65 percent base compensation and 35 percent commission. This performance orientation is particularly true of salespeople, who prefer to have as much as 38 percent of their compensation based upon commissions, which vary as a function of their sales.

The majority of employees prefer a variable as opposed to a fixed commission based on the buyer (that is, direct user versus distributor) and the nature of the product. These people believe that the degree of technical expertise required, customer demand, degree of active involvement, and other factors are quite different for the company's various product lines. Individuals were asked to write out their reasons for assigning different commissions to different customer-product segments. A categorization of the answers given to one of these segments is presented in table 11-2.

Finally, an analysis of motivational patterns showed that the sales force as a

Table 11-2
Comments on Rationale for Differential Assignment of Commissions:
Hazlitt Corporation (Industrial Division)

Rationale	Number of Comments
Largest commission (direct user industrial)	
Most effort required, good ability necessary	13
Much active involvement necessary	14
Biggest profit to company	2
Most competition	4
Much product knowledge and technical expertise necessary	8
Smallest commission (big ticket/extraction)	
Handled more by top management	9
Customer fully knowledgeable about what items he needs and wants	7

whole tends to be predominantly security-oriented (75 percent). Such employees will not be aggressive in marketing products or in exploring new market areas. Instead, they are likely to concentrate on existing markets and clients.

Several actions were taken to react to these climate findings. To deal with the high security needs, base salary levels were increased until they were competitive with U.S. industry practice. The new compensation program was structured to the nature of each selling position, emphasizing rewards reflective of performance by taking advantage of the information developed on variable commission schedules. Communication of the new plan focused on its adequacy and fairness, while other actions were taken to improve the organization of the sales force.

Because the climate analysis of the Hazlitt Corporation was conducted to determine the best compensation program for one category of employee with a particular role in the overall operation of the company, the survey could be more precisely formulated than some others, and it could be more thorough in its investigation of the specific issues of concern.

The five case studies presented above demonstrate a range of uses to which climate analysis can be put in the evaluation of current compensation programs and the development of new ones. Climate analysis serves as a flexible tool with which to gauge employee attitudes toward compensation and benefits, the impact of compensation on the organization's operation, the readiness of an organization for a specific type of compensation program, and the most productive way of meeting the compensation needs of a particular group of employees.

Motivating and Developing Key Staff Managers—
United Diversity

While the previous studies on motivation focused on compensation issues, the study conducted for United Diversity examined the question of motivation more broadly. Here the issue was to determine what types of actions would provide a long-term motivating climate for key high-level staff specialists. Allied to this question was that of how the company can assure qualified successors for these positions when they become open.

United Diversity is a multibillion-dollar U.S.-based corporation which operates worldwide and in a broad spectrum of businesses. As one of the leading companies in America, its top-level staff specialists play an important role beyond their specific job accountabilities. In forming legislation, federal and state legislators at times consult with these individuals in order to draw on their technical expertise. Policies set within this company frequently become accepted American business practices. By their very positions, top-level staff specialists often assume leadership of nationwide professional organizations.

Thus, United Diversity believes that it is critical to have individuals with a great deal of technical depth in its top staff positions. Yet this policy leads to at least two potential problems. The first is how to keep these individuals motivated when in effect they have reached the top of their career ladder. The second is now to assure that there will be qualified replacements available when the present incumbents leave the company, either through anticipated retirement or for other reasons.

The basic design of the study was to collect data through interviews and questionnaires from a series of important groups. The central group consisted of twenty-nine people in a variety of high-level staff positions. Some of these were considered "high specialists" and some of them were viewed more as "passing through" these positions on their way to general corporate management positions. A group of seven corporate vice presidents to whom these people reported were also interviewed. Finally, discussions were held with individuals in similar positions in major U.S. firms. All interviews focused on the career patterns of high-level specialists and attitudes and perceptions of jobs and working environments.

One of the first findings was that the company had not developed a definitive set of criteria to define an incumbent in a position as a "high specialist." Thus, the matrix shown in figure 11-7 was used for the purposes of the study. An incumbent who failed to meet any three of the criteria was not considered a high specialist. Fully meeting criteria 2, 4, 5, and 7 ensured inclusion. Partially meeting all criteria was sufficient, as long as any two of numbers 2, 4, and 5 were fully met. Using these decision rules, a total of sixty

	Fully meets criterion	Partly meets criterion	Fails to meet criterion
1. Consistent career development pattern			
2. Immediate supervisor unable to supervise technically			
3. Probably a terminal position			
4. Recognized as expert inside and outside company			
5. Specialty of outstanding importance to company			
6. Manages specialists in his field			
7. Difficult to replace			

Figure 11-7. United Diversity—Criteria for Identification of a Top-Level Specialist

high specialist positions in the five external companies and fourteen in United Diversity were identified.

After the high specialists were identified, an effort was made to differentiate them on the basis of their personal backgrounds and perceptions of their job environments by transcribing the interview information into forty-seven categorized items. However, on none of these items were the high specialists reliably differentiated from the remaining group of corporate staff members. Thus, surprisingly, the group identified as high-level specialists has backgrounds that are indistinguishable from those of their other staff counterparts, and they perceive the climate in which they work in much the same way. Furthermore, although the high specialist jobs are seen as taking longer to master than the others, the incumbents who were interviewed do not consider the training of a replacement to be a problem. Almost all believe that they can be replaced adequately by someone from within or outside of the company. In particular, they see no difficulty in finding someone with an appropriate degree of knowledge.

Although incumbents believe that the high specialist positions do not require a long period of tutelage, many of these jobs are filled by people with a great deal of experience who are recognized as experts in their field. Why this situation existed was still the central puzzle. Our suspicion at this point was that the reason lay in the interaction between the people who fill the positions and the requirements of the positions themselves. Therefore, the next area of inquiry was to try to understand the high specialist phenomenon through the psychology of the people involved.

The inquiry focused on motivation and used as a premise the theory advanced by Abraham Maslow, which states that people are motivated by a hierarchy of internal needs.[1] These needs are hierarchical insofar as each must be reasonably satisfied before the next is significant in directing behavior. These needs, as modified by Lyman Porter, move from security to social fulfillment, self-esteem, autonomy, and finally self-actualization, the state in which one's abilities are utilized to the greatest extent possible.[2]

In reality, these needs tend to blend with one another. At any given time, a person might be motivated by a combination of needs in different degrees. For example, an individual may be motivated primarily by social needs, that is, the needs to be affiliated with and to help others. However, he may also have active needs for security and emerging needs for self-esteem. This type of person will primarily seek situations in which he can work with or help others, but he will also tend to act in ways that will enhance his security and the recognition he receives.

Although this theory is hierarchical in nature, it should not be assumed that "high" is good and "low" is bad. Different jobs have different demands, which can be met best by people responding to different needs. The important factor is how well the individual's needs fit within the demands and potential rewards of the work climate.

A brief questionnaire at the end of each interview provided a gross measure of the area of the hierarchy with which each person associated his needs. From these results, all interviewees within United Diversity were classified as being motivated primarily by lower- or higher-order needs. These results were then compared with information that we had gained on respondents' feelings about their jobs. Two groups were identified. The people in Group 1 are basically satisfied in their jobs and receive a great deal of intrinsic reward from the content of those jobs. Those in Group 2 are motivated by the content of their jobs, but feel that their satisfaction will continue only if the jobs continue to expand or if they are able to obtain other, broader jobs. The comparison of the motivation scores for these two groups and the vice presidents is presented in figure 11-8.

Group 1 turned out to be most oriented toward needs for security, social fulfillment, and self-esteem. Career staff positions provide the opportunities to satisfy such needs, because they tend to offer more security than operating jobs with high primary accountability and they fulfill a role of helping others. Those in Group 2, as well as the vice presidents, are most motivated by needs for autonomy and self-actualization. This portion of the staff group also feels less readily replaceable than the first group, and for those in this category, outside

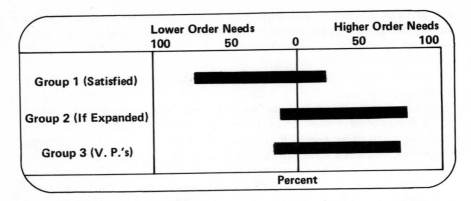

Figure 11-8. United Diversity—Percentage of Each Group Oriented Toward Higher- and Lower-Order Needs

activities, such as industry organizations and governmental contacts, play a much more important role. The reason may be that as these individuals look for expanded challenges, their efforts lead them to extend their influence outward.

Several inferences can be made about the individuals in the second group. Their job motivations are more like those of typical operating managers than of staff experts, but their career routes are different from those of operating managers. Early in their careers they entered a field of specialty and pursued a well-defined subspecialty. In their career development, they have utilized the opportunities for a rapid move to a significant position via the corporate staff route, for significant thinking challanges and wide freedom to explore new areas, for dealing with a wide range of people both within and outside of the company, and for achieving power through expert status.

However, these individuals have advanced as far organizationally as their chosen route will allow, although their basic needs lead them to seek the expanded challenges often associated with top-level operating positions. The way to satisfaction and positive motivation for this group is to expand their positions to the greatest possible degree. But two factors may stand in the way of taking this route. Additional activities for the job may not be available, and the individuals may not be able to integrate significant additions to their positions effectively.

Obviously, an understanding of the motivations and managerial talents of high-level specialists is the key to creating an appropriate climate for them. It was concluded that those specialists who are not content to view their present positions as career peaks should be given additional accountabilities which will expand their positions and maintain their high motivational levels. This route is possible in a number of instances in this company through relatively minor reorganizations. To the degree that such expansion is not possible, these people will eventually feel a reduced sense of challenge and a concomitant rise in dissatisfaction. If their skills warrant it, they might be directed into more general line positions, since this would fit more with their motivations.

It was found that the company's compensation practices for its staff specialists are competitive with other large, progressive companies and slightly more favorable than the company's overall compensation picture. However, it still might be appropriate to offer specialists an even higher base salary in exchange for an equitably reduced opportunity to participate in the company's incentive compensation program. This change would be justified on the grounds that specialists' accountabilities are generally of a long-term, institutional nature, and it would provide some recognition of that unique type of impact.

Because titles were found to be an important form of recognition for the individuals who were motivated to increase their accountabilities, the company could consider changing its current conservative practice of narrowly restricting the use of the "vice president" designation. Other companies give equivalent specialists in their organizations titles similar to "staff vice president." Such a designation could be used for the broader jobs among the staff specialists.

Finally, the study did not find replacement to be a major problem. Given a forced choice, it would be more advisable for the company to go to outside sources for specialists than to attempt to stockpile potential replacements in line. In many cases it might be easier and more effective to restructure a function than to seek an exact replacement for some individual's unique combination of talents and experience. An attempt to provide continuity with outside contacts should be initiated by an explicit policy of encouraging the introduction and continuing involvement of both peers and younger specialists in the network of high specialist contacts.

While this study did not approach climate measurement in the more traditional manner cited in most of the other cases, it did devise a methodology for eliciting quantifiable information concerning the activities, perceptions, and values of the individuals involved. This was then analyzed in a variety of ways until an understanding of the dynamics of the problem and, finally, a set of recommendations designed to maximize motivation and utilization were produced.

Notes

1. Abraham H. Maslow, *Motivation and Personality* (New York: Harper & Row, 1954), p. 69.

2. Lyman W. Porter, "Job Attitudes in Management: I. Perceived Deficiencies in Need Fulfillment as a Function of Job Level," *Journal of Applied Psychology* 46 (December 1962):375-384.

12 Manpower Development

Climate analysis can play an effective role in the formulation of manpower development programs in at least two ways: as a tool to measure the effects of organizational climate in enhancing or retarding the advancement of employees, and as a tool to define the characteristics of successful performance in certain positions so that new talent can be developed to meet such criteria.

In the example discussed below, that of American Distributing, the entire operation of the organization, not just its training function, required revision to encourage the necessary management growth. Climate surveys were used before, during, and after implementation of the new program to measure its effectiveness in accomplishing its goals.

Failures of the Existing System

American Distributing, a large labor-intensive national organization engaged in shipping and delivery, suffered from antiquated methods of human resource utilization which failed to meet the needs of the managerial structure and techniques called for by its current mission. Bogged down in human and financial wastefulness, it still used methods designed for the situation of thirty years ago. The organization required modern managers who could provide modern management.

Three primary deficiencies mandated reorganization of American Distributing management, broadening of management opportunity, and development of an attitude among present and prospective employees that the company is a good place to work.

First, the traditional clerical or manual entry job had placed a unique burden for self-improvement on the individual. Horatio Alger-type success within the company was the rule rather than the exception. Nowhere else would top production, marketing, financial, and personnel managers be expected to grow from the same manual-work beginnings and acquire the refined skills necessary for their assignments through their own initiative. Unfortunately, the availability of people willing to accept this challenge and able to meet it has been insufficient since the mid-1930s, when many overqualified people were forced by the Depression to accept the unskilled positions at the entry level in American Distributing.

This problem was also the source of the second deficiency. The total system depended on the dedication of and the often overwhelming workload assumed by senior managers, whose age and length of service would make such dependence impossible in the future. Third, current management style emphasized knowledge of procedures. But business called for a change to the problem-solving, results orientation needed for the company to be self-sustaining.

Objectives and Critical Areas for Change

Given these conditions, creation of an appropriate manpower development program had to embody certain procedural guidelines. An organizational pattern of properly structured management and supervisory positions had to be established. The development process had to provide employees with opportunities for planned growth in challenging and rewarding careers and to provide American Distributing with the right person for the right job at the right time. Accomplishment of this goal depended upon a training program that could upgrade performance, put opportunity within reach, and assure an available and qualified source of manpower. Finally, climate analysis was needed to ensure that efforts actually could be directed toward the establishment of an environment that encourages achievement and advancement. Therefore, the principal objective of the manpower development project was the formulation of an attractive, motivating, and retentive careers system based on four key premises:

1. The system should provide more effective and objective ways of identifying merit and promotability.
2. It should emphasize the development of employees and encourage them to plan career objectives and prepare for promotion.
3. It should support employees' desire for practical progression in a career with integral training and development programs.
4. It should be a management tool that permits short- and long-range planning for current and future manpower needs and helps to assure adequate manpower resources.

Accomplishment of these premises depends on the effective implementation of two crucial changes, one involving results-oriented management and the other, enhancement of formal training programs.

The change to a results management orientation calls for formal professional training and individual guidance, so that the organization's total supervisory-management force achieves a working knowledge of the critical job content of subordinates' jobs, the results expected of themselves and those reporting to them, methods of objectively measuring achievement against those results, and the interrelationship of their jobs with those above, below, and at their own level. Changes in organization, management philosophy, and operating style of the company must be carried out if accountability management is to be implemented. The organizational structure must group similar functions to contribute to operating effectiveness as well as to optimize a career progression system. Information, authority for decision and actions, and other essential resources for problem resolution must be placed at appropriate organizational levels. To assure clarity and understanding of accountabilities at all levels of management, each supervisor or manager should understand the results for which he is accountable and how they affect and interrelate with the accountabilities of associated positions.

A functionally arranged structure was developed to provide the organizational environment necessary to accomplish such changes. Modifications in management philosophy and operating style to capitalize on this new structure involve managers' learning new management processes and techniques which complement the structure.

Results-oriented management relies on individual job planning, total-organization job planning and communication, and management team building. Therefore, all supervisors and managers were given training in the concepts of accountability management to enable each individual to interrelate effectively with others, so that objectives can be attained. In fact, a management process involving interrelationship of accountabilities was designed to assure integration and coordination of effort by affirming the commitment of top management to agreed-upon objectives and by achieving these objectives.

Enhancement of the formal career-training program depends upon the company's ability to provide, and its employees' willingness to undergo, training that will provide qualified people and logical promotion. The first step was an audit of available training opportunities to determine their scope and technical level. The data provided by the audit divided opportunities into two basic categories, training for different job activities at various technical levels, and training for various levels of management and human relations skills. Then specifications for the various job activities carried out throughout the organization were compared to the list of training programs developed during the audit. For those activities that lacked such training, a recommendation was made for the establishment of a program.

The career development system that emerged was founded on the principle of similarity of job content and stressed logical movement between jobs. It made provisions for the individual in a position to be competently trained to handle the critical elements of that position, and it accounted for accurate, objective assessment of employees' skills and strengths for career advancement. Utilization of the system for career development by employees was also stressed, as were the manpower needs of management.

This installation of completely new management and career processes meant a radical alteration in the characteristics of the organization. Of course, these changes will only produce the desired results if they have a significant effect upon the behavior of individuals. Therefore, climate analysis was used to measure managers' perceptions of these changes and the resulting effect on job satisfaction, performance, motivation, and commitment to careers.

Role of Climate Analysis

An understanding of organizational climate is particularly significant for this project because of its implications concerning stimulation of employee behavior, satisfaction of employee needs, enhancement of career opportunities, and interrelationships of people. An initial survey was made to aid in the formulation of recommendations for change, a second survey indicated reactions to some of the early change activities, and a third survey measured the effects of these changes after their implementation.

The initial survey pointed to two key issues. The differences between personal needs for responsibility and achievement were very large. Although the responses indicated strong desires for achievement and its commensurate stature, individuals had little desire to accept the responsibility that goes along with it. In addition, the degree to which people felt encouraged to work toward difficult results, termed "press for performance," was quite low. The need to correct these problems played a central role in the recommendations for change.

The second survey showed a number of desirable results during the process of change. It revealed that people perceived a good deal of available opportunity and believed that advancement was based on performance, which their immediate supervisors were able to appraise accurately. These positive findings enhanced the possibility that results-oriented management could take hold in the organization.

However, some specific problem areas were also noted. The lack of achievement orientation continued. When people considered what they could do to facilitate their own advancement, they thought in terms of general performance and gave very little mention of formal training or gathering of new experience through lateral transfer. The finding of a notable resistance to change led to the use of intensive individual counseling to establish the concepts of performance planning and measurement.

At the time of the third survey, the organizational structure had been changed, including the movement of a number of people into different jobs. Incumbents had become familiar with their accountabilities and had received counseling in defining specific goals, standards, and measures. Yet people were still feeling the impact of the recent personnel changes and were not comfortable in their new situations. As expected in this circumstance, the results reflected both their view of the future and their reactions to the recent past.

As indicated in table 12-1, the group questioned saw about the same promotional opportunities as it had in the second survey, when the implementation project started. However, an indirect question used in the survey may be a

Table 12-1
Attitudes Toward Future Career Opportunities: American Distributing

	Percent Responses	
	2nd Survey	3rd Survey
Many opportunities	13	19
Limited, but available	59	53
Few opportunities	22	22
Almost nonexistent	5	7

better indicator of impact. Here, people were asked to write their own answers when asked what actions they could take to increase their chances for advancement. The concern was to elicit the degree to which people saw training and the obtaining of different job experiences as vehicles to promotion. The hypothesis was that the new activities to define accountabilities and develop a career-path program would make people more aware of these avenues, as opposed to their merely doing their jobs well.

As indicated in table 12-2, the hypothesis seems to be correct, with the proportion indicating the advantage of some type of personal development rising from 40 to 54 percent. Since this question called for spontaneous responses and since the shifts in responses are clear, it is evident that supervisors and managers within the company were becoming more oriented toward thinking in terms of specific actions that would make them more valuable to American Distributing in the future.

Figure 12-1 presents further data on some of the questions that addressed central objectives of the project. In each case, only slight differences exist between responses on the first two surveys, but a substantial rise occurs on the third. This sequence of results indicates that perceptions are sensitive to "real"

Table 12-2
Attitudes Toward the Type of Actions Required for Future Advancement: American Distributing

	Percent Responses	
	2nd Survey	3rd Survey
Training	36	46
New job experiences	4	8
Total Development Related	40	54
General performance	36	25
Non-job-related	12	9
None	12	12
Total Nondevelopment Related	60	46

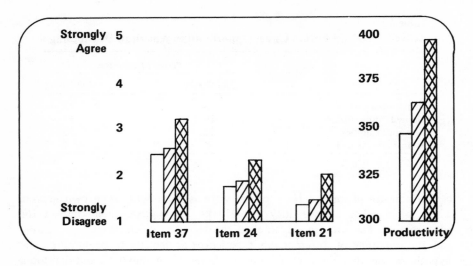

Item 37: There is pressure here to improve your performance.
Item 24: Training people to take on bigger jobs is a way of life here.
Item 21: We have a promotion system that helps the best person to rise
          to the top.

☐ February 1970
▨ June 1970
▨ May 1971

Figure 12-1. American Distributing—Changes in Perceptions and Performance

change. Between the first two surveys, the major activity had been in communicating the changes that would take place and providing seminars in performance planning and measurement. Yet the company was still being run in fundamentally the same way as it had been before the project started. People had not yet lived with change. By the time of the third survey, change was more than talk. People were in new position, their daily activities were now related to individual performance plans, and many were involved in some type of specific developmental activity. Thus, their reactions to pressure, training, or promotion were now based on real events.

Interestingly, as figure 12-1 suggests, performance of the organization improved as the climate became more oriented toward excellence. The last set of lines presents a measure of overall production deemed to be the most representative of organizational performance. While a 4.9 percent rise in performance was experienced during the first phase of the project, a 9.4 percent rise was attained during the second. These figures are quite similar to the changes in climate perceptions.

13 Management by Objectives

The various approaches to results-oriented management, or management by objectives (MBO), constitute one of the most significant movements in managerial processes in recent years. As more and more organizations attempt to adopt and extend these concepts, climate considerations take on a special importance. Because management by objectives often represents a profound change in an organization's operational style, careful attention must be paid to management perceptions of the demands, rewards, and relationships within the organization, for difficulties associated with these perceptions are among the greatest obstacles to instituting change.

Management by objectives coordinates the entire operation of an organization, stressing the cooperative role of people at various levels. As a participative program, it attempts to influence the future rather then react to situations as they arise. By focusing on goals and how to achieve them, it can contribute to planning, decision-making, and the specific contributions made by individuals. The basic goals of the organization are translated into objectives that are understandable in the context of day-to-day operations, that provide guidance and controls for those operations, and that coordinate individual activities.

Theoretically, the individual participates in setting the objectives for his own job, and those goals determine the nature and scope of the job's activities as they relate to unit and organizational goals. Through this process, the individual better understands the organization's overall objectives, his role in the organization, and his contribution to achieving the overall goals. Better relationships among individuals at various levels are encouraged because people become aware of how their work interrelates. Communication improves because it is vital to the interaction of individuals and units. The key impact of MBO for individuals is better motivation and a sense of accomplishment.

These advantages of results-oriented management are, of course, ideal ones, benefits that are possible if the situation within an organization is right. One of the most important considerations of that situation is whether the climate will enhance or retard adaptation of what is usually a major change in operational philosophy.

Introducing a new management concept which challenges long-established habits and ideas is not easily accomplished under the best of circumstances. The greatest mistake possible for any innovator is to underestimate the resistance to change that he will encounter. Probably the principal shortcoming in actual operation of MBO has been the frequent failure of those introducing the system to take into account the present climate and what type of motivations that climate stimulates, for the motivations of those people who are actually accountable for running the various parts of the organization will lead them to embrace or reject the innovation. If the current climate encourages innovative, risk-oriented behavior, one can anticipate that by either selection or attrition, the organization will have a large proportion of individuals whose motivations are consistent with such behaviors. If, on the other hand, the climate discourages such behaviors, one can expect to find a large number of individuals who are security-oriented and would view significant change as a threat to the status quo.

Because MBO is such a pervasive influence on the management system, it is important to have a clear understanding of motivational patterns, mission, and current climate before implementation. By looking at these three factors, management can then take definitive steps to create the climate that will enhance the relationship between the individual and the organization to produce the most positive results for both.

Climate Issues

Basic data on an organization's potential for achieving such a relationship and on the problems that must be overcome beforehand can be obtained by focusing on certain elements of the standard climate dimensions: the quality of management systems, the quality of cooperation and coordination, the quality of rewards, and the quality of challenge. These are central considerations for the kind of employee performance essential to a results orientation.

An unusual opportunity to determine the relationship of management climate and organizational performance occurred recently in a comprehensive study conducted in a large multilocation distributing organization (Zenith Distributing) where each location was both self-contained and similar to others. Because this study was undertaken to improve management effectiveness, issues relevant to management by objectives were considered.

Since each location had the same basic function (receiving, routing, and shipping its products) and operated under a highly developed set of rules and procedures, it was widely assumed that climate would show little variance from one installation to another. However, even within the severe constraints imposed, clear differences emerged, reflecting an array of management styles.

In the early stages of the study, managers at eight locations were surveyed concerning their working climates. The survey measured five distinct areas of climate, not unlike the dimensions discussed earlier, at each location:

1. The degree to which managers felt they were encouraged to innovate in their jobs.
2. The degree to which managers felt personally involved in the management process.

3. The degree to which different units within each location cooperated and communicated in getting the overall job done.
4. The degree to which the management process was structured and covered by procedures.
5. The degree to which managers were encouraged to meet clear and challenging performance standards.

Figure 13-1 indicates climate and productivity in two of the eight locations. The vertical bars represent the rank of the location on each climate factor; the higher the bar, the higher the location ranks on the factor. The horizontal line represents an independent productivity measure of each location, compiled by

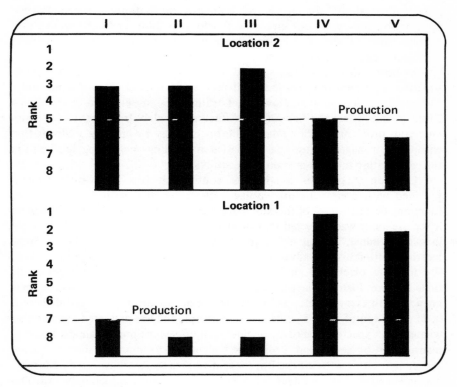

I — Innovation
II — Involvement
III — Cooperation
IV — Degree of Procedure
V — Press for Performance

Figure 13-1. Zenith Distributing—Climate and Productivity in Two Locations

the company through a complex standard work measurement system. It measures how well each location performs as a whole in moving its products through the system, rather than the output of any individual.

On innovation, involvement, and cooperation, the first location is very low. On degree of procedure and performance demand, it is very high. But actual performance is near the bottom. This is almost a stereotyped profile of an authoritarian management style. Therefore, it came as little surprise to learn that every morning the general manager of that location held a staff meeting to discuss in detail what happened the previous day—in effect, a management "show and tell." When managers were interviewed to determine the qualities they believed to be most important in management climate, they inevitably began by pulling out a sheet of figures. Although this authoritarian style created tremendous pressure for performance, it failed to achieve results because the general manager did not tap the more creative motivations of the employees. Specifically, they were not given the freedom to think or the freedom to act beyond narrow limits. The general manager attempted to control all problem-solving and issued orders to cover all eventualities.

At times this method may succeed with a small work force, in an emergency situation, or where the organizational process does not fluctuate significantly and problems are minimal. However, Location 1 is an operation of more than 2,000 people where the flow of work fluctuates widely from day to day, with numerous problems requiring daily adjustment. Only by creating a climate that encourages managers to use their initiative in adapting to changing demands can the organization meet its mission successfully.

Location 2 presents a complete contrast. It is a newly-built facility, provided with every currently available electronic and mechanical aid for its function. Because of all of this automation and the enormous capital investment it represents, it was expected that production would be at the top of the eight locations studied. But, as indicated in figure 13-1, it fell in the middle. Some locations with much less advanced facilities actually had higher output.

In terms of climate, the second location shows an opposite pattern to the first. It scores high on participation, innovation, and cooperation. Everyone gets on well with everyone else and shares in the management process. But there is little definition of what is expected from people and less pressure to ensure that whatever is expected is actually achieved. In effect, the process almost becomes management by abdication. People are encouraged to innovate, show initiative, and communicate with others. But these attributes are not balanced by adequate demands and control, as evidenced in the relatively poor production record. This location suffers from an overemphasis on personal needs and an underemphasis on organizational needs, resulting in a serious imbalance.

Both locations, despite their differences, would present significant climate obstacles to the implementation of a system of management by objectives. However, understanding where an organization stands on these and other related climate issues provides considerable guidance in determining the effort needed to achieve a new management system. Finally, understanding the nature of the motivations of its people completes the picture of how far and how fast the organization can move in a new direction. With this information, management can implement the program in a way that will blend with and move forward from the current state of functioning.

Implementing Management by Objectives

The first necessary consideration is a determination of how readily people will accept change. The authoritarian situation of Location 1 is illustrative of an organization that needs a long preparation period. Two steps are essential. The individual at the top must be replaced, or his views of the management process must be changed. Such a change will not occur simply by his adoption of new goals, measures, and standards. Rather, some type of organizational development process aimed at behavioral change will have to be implemented. The second step involves preparation of his subordinates to accept accountability—probably a lengthy process, since they have operated under a restrictive system for so long and have developed a very strong security orientation. Indeed, managers in Location 1 rated the assumption of responsibility as their least important need, a phenomenon quite different from that revealed in the higher-performing locations.

In a situation where conflict exists among those reporting to the top manager, a management-by-objectives program should not be begun until all are prepared to work as a team toward organizational goals. Results-oriented management would have to be preceded by an organizational development process to weld these people into an effective team. Location 2, in contrast, is an example of an organization prepared for more immediate implementation of MBO. The groundwork of involvement and coordination and the focus on performance of the MBO process will solve many of the organization's problems.

The system can work from the top down, with superiors formulating goals for subordinates, or goal-setting and development of measures can be a joint process, with substantial negotiation between management levels. The degree to which people are motivated to take individual responsibility is the determining factor of how much participation will work best. Do people want a structured situation in which they are accountable mainly for implementing plans developed above? Or would they perform best in a situation where they can have wide latitude in which to operate but are held accountable for broad results? In many instances, people strongly resist utilizing the authority available to them.

Experience has shown that a successful way to introduce management by objectives to individuals who have not been accustomed to accepting responsibility is to break up the accountabilities into small, specific elements. In other words, the scope of expected accomplishment is narrow, but the performance of each element is still delegated without specifying the means by which it is accomplished.

One of the key decisions involved in implementing a management-by-objective system is to determine where and when emphasis should be placed. While the development of performance measures, the setting of goals, and the specifying of various levels or standards of performance against goals are all part of MBO, initial emphasis may be placed on one or another of these elements. For example, if a climate analysis indicates that people are unaccustomed to accountability, it would be more appropriate to place initial emphasis on developing measures of performance, with the development of standards based on these measures coming later. This approach would enable the system to grow initially through a planning and development process, with the later inclusion of a performance evaluation component.

Basically, a question exists as to how threatening the new system will be to those who have to operate within it. Will managers be primarily concerned with looking forward to accomplishing goals? Or will they be more concerned that they will be under surveillance by superiors, who are checking on their accomplishment of planned objectives?

The primary purpose of MBO is to provide an organization with the framework for planned performance. In some environments, this purpose is best accomplished by concentrating on measures that will aid in planning and subsequently in monitoring the adopted plans realistically. As people gain confidence in the validity of the measures, those measures may then be used as the base for developing standards for individual performance evaluation.

Because many differences exist among organizations, because MBO represents a profound influence on the management way of life, and because so many possible methods of developing this life exist, a critical requirement for any organization is that it have a thorough understanding of itself so that it can adopt in a planned, productive manner the way of life that is best for it. Successful introduction of a results-oriented management system into an organization can be enhanced greatly if both the design of the system and the method of introduction take into account the existing organizational climate.

14 External Influences

Although management climate has been defined as an internal phenomenon, it often has important external implications. Furthermore, the same survey techniques that are employed in climate analysis can be applied to appropriate external populations in order to obtain their perceptions of various functions of an organization. Such populations may include customers, suppliers, the general public, legislators, and many others. Although the external climate (defined as the perceptions of such populations) may not affect the organization's operation as directly and immediately as the internal one does, it is highly significant for at least two major reasons. First, the actions of others toward the organization may be felt directly in terms of sales volume, legislative restrictions, opposition to expansion plans, and so forth. Second, how employees *believe* that the outside world perceives the organization is a major factor in decisions affecting actions toward that world. In this case, just as in the case of internal climate, perceptions rather than realities will often have the greater influence on management actions.

Market Images of an Engine Manufacturer

The Burlingham Engine Company had gone through a very traumatic period in its history. Having been one of the pioneers in its field, it has a well-recognized name and position in providing equipment to a variety of industries, including manufacturing, utilities, petroleum extraction, and shipbuilding. Some years ago, the company was acquired by a major manufacturing firm, and during the past ten years it has encountered major problems in financial performance, product competitiveness, manufacturing efficiency, and other areas of internal management. In response to this situation, the chairman and president of the company were replaced, a new sense of purpose was communicated, and reorganization of products and facilities was accomplished. Within two years, the profitability of the company, while not leading the industry, had become respectable.

At this point, the top management of the firm conducted a climate study to determine whether the new structures and systems that they had installed were operating appropriately down through the levels of management. A total discussion of the results of that study would be redundant with many of the other cases that we have discussed. One aspect, however, leads into an area thus far unexplored: In particular, executives were asked to provide their own

159

perceptions of how customers and potential customers viewed various aspects of Burlingham.

Figure 14-1 presents the results of one element of that inquiry. Ratings are quite consistent among different functions of the company, placing the company's product quality and reliability in the "good" to "excellent" range.

How do you think customers would rate Burlingham in the following areas?

Figure 14-1. Burlingham Engine Company—Executive Impressions of Customer Images

Backing up those products with technical support is seen as somewhat less positive, but still very close to an overall "good" rating. Some disagreement exists over the customer image of delivery time, but overall ratings are not favorable, varying around the "fair" category. Finally, the company's pricing is also viewed as a weak point, receiving ratings close to the "fair" level on competitiveness.

Top management had two major reactions to these results. The first was that the people who produced the product, manufacturing and engineering and research, had significantly different views on deliverability than did those who worked with the customer (sales and marketing). It was felt that the standards accepted by the producers might not be adequate for the demands of the marketplace. Second, top management believed the company to be in the same price range as its competitors, if not lower. However, the fact that most managers believe that the buying world considers Burlingham to be a relatively high-priced supplier will cause an unwarranted defensiveness on the part of sales and marketing and the possibility that engineering and research will be unduly oriented toward sacrificing quality in order to lower price.

To help clarify and deal with these issues, top management commissioned a further series of studies to determine how the marketplace *actually* viewed Burlingham. Two parallel studies were conducted. One was a mail survey of customers who had had recent contact with the sales force. This study investigated a number of questions concerning the knowledge and practices of the sales force in addition to the issues of price, reliability, and delivery of the company's products. The second was a phone survey of design engineers and purchasing agents representative of ten separate markets served by the company. In this study, the sponsor was unidentified and people were asked to respond to questions about each of the major companies in the field.

Figure 14-2 presents results from all three studies, placed on the same scale for comparison purposes. The external studies support the executive perceptions in terms of the relative strengths and weaknesses of the four factors. Indeed, customers and potential customers believe Burlingham to have a high-quality, reliable product backed up by better-than-average technical support. On the other hand, delivery time is seen as worse than average, especially by the general market of buyers, rather than just those who had made purchases from Burlingham and were therefore more committed to the company. Thus, delivery time appeared to be a more critical problem than recognized by manufacturing and engineering. In fact, of the three major companies in the industry, Burlingham received the lowest ratings on delivery time (figure 14-3).

On the question of price competitiveness, Burlingham is seen as very close to average, a view that is more favorable than that held by most company executives and certainly more favorable than that of Burlingham's marketing executives. Thus, to some extent, the company's top management was correct in gauging price competitiveness.

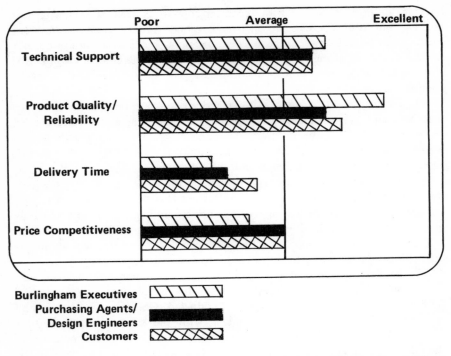

Figure 14-2. Burlingham Engine Company—Competitive Image From Three Perspectives

Testing the external realities of internal perceptions led in this case to some very clear directions for internal action. The easiest was to use the results of the surveys to conduct a strong internal communications program to the marketing and sales force about the pricing structure of Burlingham relative to that of the industry. Greater emphasis could be placed upon Burlingham's ability to deliver higher quality and support at a competitive price.

The more difficult action is to raise the engineering and manufacturing standards relative to delivery time. The company had already taken a number of steps to overcome bottlenecks in manufacturing, but the survey clearly indicated that the results had not yet put it into a competitive posture in this area, despite the fact that neither Burlingham nor the industry was producing at capacity. It was evident that major managerial attention was necessary to enhance delivery performance.

Introducing a New Banking Service

A second example of the usefulness of comparing internal to external perceptions comes from a study in which one of the issues investigated was the

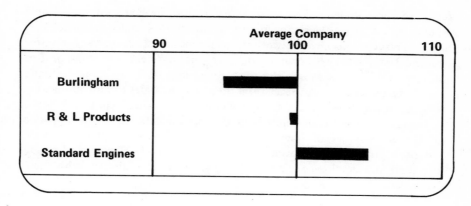

Figure 14-3. Burlingham Engine Company—Comparison of the Three Major Companies on Delivery Time

possibility of introducing various automated facilities in a large, urban bank system. Here sixty-nine bankers were questioned about their attitudes toward various aspects of automated banking. Then this same group was asked to answer the same questions in the way that they believed customers would answer them, a process called role-playing. Finally, 251 actual customers were surveyed on the same questions. Each group was asked the extent to which they agreed or disagreed with statements such as

"Machines have made banking too complicated for most people to understand."

"If banks used more machines, I wouldn't have to wait in teller lines so long."

"Bank computers and machines handle my money more safely than people would."

The results of these surveys were quite dramatic. As indicated in table 14-1, customers and bankers agreed very closely in their attitudes toward automation.

Table 14-1
Agreement in Attitudes Toward Automated Banking

Relationship Between	Correlation
Customers and bankers	.91[a]
Customers and bankers (role-playing)	.17
Bankers and bankers (role-playing)	−.07

[a]Statistically significant level ($p < .01$).

Yet when these same bankers were asked to describe how customers would respond, they changed their answers very significantly—so much so, in fact, that there was no real agreement between them and the actual customers. Answering for themselves, the bankers' own reactions were not different from those of their customers. However, as those responsible for making decisions about customer services, the bankers did not react from their own attitudes toward automation but from a totally false perception of how customers would accept such services.

The cases of the Burlingham Engine Company and the urban bank provide two diverse examples of how the perceptions of external publics can be investigated profitably to provide perspective for internal climate studies and information for developing plans for actions that deal directly with these publics.

15 Effective Climate Management

A management climate survey is not an end in itself. Rather, it is a first step that helps to target attention on significant areas of management concern. Therefore, the climate analysis process does not stop once the survey findings are in. In fact, one of management's greatest challenges lies in developing programs to deal positively and effectively with survey results.

Recently, representatives of four companies that have employed climate analysis presented their approaches to mounting and sustaining climate improvement efforts to an audience of senior personnel executives. Their experiences indicate that while each organization's situation is unique, certain principles are valid across situations and of value to any program to achieve more effective climate management. Five major principles emerged from their discussion:

1. Climate results must be translated into specific company issues. Management must address the question of what company policies, practices, or structures led to the survey results. Although these results are an excellent means of focusing on the right issues, truly significant change cannot occur until results are related to the conditions that produced them.

2. Functionally, the accountability for assuring an effective management climate rests with the human resource executive. While most actions necessary to create an effective climate are line responsibilities, the personnel executive must first assure that operating officers have the tools needed to manage their climate, and then follow up to see that they are forceful and persistent in applying those tools.

3. Management climate must be measured over time. Just as financial measures track success or failure of major elements of the enterprise, climate measurements must be used to assure that specific programs are accomplishing their objectives. It is often desirable to track climate and financial results in tandem, directly relating the bottom-line orientation to management productivity.

4. The company must respond to issues uncovered by the survey. This principle does not mean that all criticism must be accepted as fact or that all problems must be solved. But a frank and complete explanation of why certain problems exist in an organization can be more effective than ill-conceived, piecemeal attempts to address an issue.

5. Survey feedback programs should involve the talents of experienced professional personnel. The communication of survey results, if carried out effectively, can be an excellent tool for building goodwill and commitment and

165

mobilizing management resources for action. If communication is poorly accomplished, however, the potency of this tool will be lost.

Regardless of the specific approaches used with survey results, painstaking care must be given to ensuring that efforts are thoroughly planned, supported by company policy-makers, and oriented to deployment and follow-through of accountabilities.

Action-Oriented Problem-Solving

One of the companies participating in the presentation, a major bank, used an action-oriented approach to deal with issues raised by the climate survey. The process involved three panels, each consisting of nine members representing a functional and hierarchical cross section of management employees. Internal human resources professionals who served as discussion facilitators enhanced panel productivity. All survey participants were encouraged to convey their thoughts to their panel representatives well in advance of the problem-solving meetings.

Working with the climate data and confidential financial operating and market data provided by top management, the panels generated twenty-four recommendations, each supported by statements of rationale, mechanics of implementation, accountability, and, where possible, projected cost-benefit ratios.

A senior bank officer concluded that panel members worked hard on the project and commended their commitment and candor. Many participants reacted positively to their involvement, and all were eager to receive top management's responses to their proposals. Nevertheless, two panels expressed a serious lack of confidence in senior management; they revealed doubts about the leadership's sincerity in initiating the panel project. One group stated that "probably nothing will come of our recommendations." Another panel, however, was enthusiastic about the purposes of the project. It supported the goal of increased productivity and profitability and expected its recommendations to have a positive effect on those areas. It set its own standard, desiring the bank to rank in the upper quartile in organizational vitality, integration, management style, and related factors.

The two recommendations discussed below are illustrative of the type of issues with which the panels dealt.

Recommendation #11: Development of a bank-wide long-range planning process is strongly encouraged. Active and candid solicitation of middle-management input and participation is advised.

The projected impact of this recommendation is a strengthening of officer morale, with a resultant renewal of commitment and excellent opportunities for training experience. The cost would be in the great number of man-hours required to make the planning effective. However, successful planning would offset this cost with the benefits of more aggressive objectives and higher morale.

In its comments, the panel was encouraged by recent developments in the areas of long-range planning, specifically, the assignment of responsibility for overall corporate planning, human resources planning, and financial planning. These developments were seen as indications that management has recognized deficiencies in the planning process and made positive moves to correct them. However, the panel's plan provided for an integration of these efforts, their extension to the whole bank, and greater involvement of middle management.

Recommendation #7: Develop better management skills in senior management.

The projected impact of this recommendation is improved employee morale and performance because of courtesy, thoughtfulness, and awareness of individual needs on the part of the bank's management. Other anticipated benefits include improved employee relations, improved credibility of and respect for senior management, and minimized frustrations. The costs involved would be primarily in the time required for senior managers to attend in-house or externally sponsored programs in basic human relations.

The comments behind the recommendation included a strong statement that "continuation of an aloof, detached, and rude attitude on the part of certain members of senior management is resulting in needless officer turnover, lowered morale, and a feeling of frustration on the part of many officers." Others concluded that contributions to the panel from all areas of the bank emphasized this problem and that it has led to widespread apathy. Senior management's failure to encourage genuine communication was noted.

Other recommendations included establishment of an incentive compensation system, a review of the adequacy of staffing, increases in staff, establishment of a management communications council, and improvement in certain benefit plans. Top management's policy committee reviewed each recommendation, concentrating on creating action plans for workable solutions and providing candid explanations to the panels for those recommendations judged to be infeasible. The bank's representative concluded that the positive changes stimulated by the climate survey program have exerted a far-reaching effect on the bank, one that is much greater than that of an organizational development program that had been in operation for a number of years.

The Commitment to Change

The commitment to improve management climate is not necessarily the result of an immediate decision. The example of a major metals producer shows that the building of top management commitment can be an evolutionary process spanning a number of years.

The organization functions on a decentralized basis with six operating units, each having a profit and loss accountability. The company is growing rapidly, along with its basic industry, and is enjoying significant capital investment. Three climate studies surveyed approximately 200 of the highest-level managers and executives in a work force of 6,000.

Although at the time of the first survey (in 1974) results were communicated downward and some reactions moved upward in an unorganized manner, the changes that were recommended to improve climate were either ignored or deferred. Because senior management had not really accepted the concept of a climate survey, and therefore its results, little credence was given to the survey and as a result nothing was accomplished.

Changes were made in the procedure for the second survey in 1975, in hopes of establishing greater credibility. In general, results were just a little worse than those of the previous year, except in compensation. Communication occurred, responses were developed, and recommendations were made. But again they were ignored. Managers were still not ready to accept climate analysis as a management tool. In fact, no survey was conducted in 1976.

The 1977 survey was approached with a great deal of trepidation. Not only had no progress been made in achieving positive results, but the general picture conveyed by the survey data was one of some deterioration since 1975. After three climate surveys, each showing a slightly worsening situation, management realized that something was wrong. Despite the favorable situation of the company and its excellent operating results in the period from 1974 to 1977, the climate trend was in an opposite direction. The company decided that it would not be able to maintain or improve its record with a deteriorating management climate.

The seriousness of the company's dilemma climaxed a long campaign to involve its executives in "the people side of the business." The 1977 climate results verified predictions made after the 1974 survey. Management was finally committed to change.

In retrospect, the results of the previous surveys were not totally wasted. But it had taken several years for the company to accept them and resolve to do something about them. Once the president and senior management decided to change the climate, human resources personnel developed a plan to accomplish this goal. The strategy included several objectives: pinpointing two or three key problem areas and priority issues for the company in general and for each of six operating areas, defining action plans to respond to these issues, and developing procedures to review these plans to assure their success.

All climate survey participants were oriented through the communication of survey results in three categories: matters that could be corrected, matters that would require further study, and matters that were beyond management's control. Then feedback sessions were held with senior management so that they could agree on the nature of the issues to be confronted and be involved actively in the resolution of those issues. A similar process was conducted on the level of each unit, first to obtain reaction to the climate results and then to develop action plans. At the end of the sessions, the action plans were communicated in writing. As a follow-up, a performance contact concept was introduced for implementation between the president and the general manager of each unit. This concept proved to be the crucial element in the commitment to change.

The communications strategy produced two priority issues for the company, dealing with performance orientation and human resource development. These issues also applied to the units, along with specific unit problems. Both company and unit management developed performance commitments to bring about improvements.

While the process is well under way and outcomes are still not specific, a noticeable change seems to have taken place within the company. More lateral movement of personnel for developmental purposes, a change in the compensation program, greater willingness to confront difficult personnel decisions, and a very dramatic increase in profit objectives are all part of the new, emerging climate.

Unfortunately, management did not give its attention to climate survey results for several years, until it could not help but be disturbed by the 1977 findings. But once it accepted the need for change, the leadership spent considerable time on reviewing the results and developing action plans, an effort that is already benefiting the company.

Monitoring Climate Over Time

The example of the metals producer shows how important it is for an organization to be aware of the conditions of its climate over time, just as it has a crucial need to be aware of inventory, projected sales and costs, cash flow, and available financial resources. However, business recognition of the critical importance of keeping informed about the continuing internal state of the organization has lagged far behind a corresponding awareness of the need for financial data.

Assessment of changes in the managerial climate over time permits management to track the development of certain climate characteristics and, more important, to evaluate the effectiveness of attempts to improve the climate. Appreciable periods are often required before a particular program or strategy has an impact on results. Therefore, trends in the relationships among newly implemented programs, managerial climate, and results must be described fully for a lengthy period before cause-and-effect conclusions can be formulated.

A large field experiment conducted in a national service company demonstrates the importance of looking at results over time.[1] In this instance, a program designed to improve supervision was instituted in an experimental department within the company. The original expectation was that significant changes in management style would result in productivity gain within six months. However, while measurements at the end of the six-month period revealed the beginning of improvement in perceptions, attitudes, and motivation, an additional year was required for significant changes in productivity to occur. This finding is very similar to the results of a case study we reported in chapter 12. The productivity increase in comparison to control groups was both substantial and enduring. This experiment shows that the impact of change may not be reflected in results for appreciable periods of time.

On the other hand, immediate gains in organizational productivity following the implementation of a program may not be indicative of a completely healthy situation. In fact, research has demonstrated that while typical cost-reduction procedures such as tightening hierarchical control, increasing pressure for productivity, lowering cost through personnel limitations, cutting budgets, and tightening work standards may bring immediate improvements in productivity and costs, these improvements tend to hide the development of unfavorable climate trends for some period of time.[2]

The negative impact of an unhealthy managerial climate on variables such as productivity, costs, and earnings may not be felt for an extended period. While it is difficult to predict exactly when the effects will become apparent, various trouble signs will certainly appear beforehand. For example, increased resentment of unreasonable hierarchical pressure for increased production and reduced costs may be accompanied by a sharp decline in confidence and trust in top management. Upward and downward communications are likely to become more filtered and distorted. The resulting loss in accuracy of the information available for the organization's decision-makers will produce signs of deterioration in the decision-making processes. Quality of services and products may begin to suffer and, consequently, so may customer loyalty.

At some point in this sequence, actual cost and productivity performance will begin to fall. However, pressure for cost reduction may remain high, further compounding the problem. Increases in labor difficulties and in turnover, along with greater waste, poorer quality, and unfavorable customer reaction, finally may force top management to reevaluate the situation and plan corrective actions. Unfortunately, substantial improvement of an extremely unfavorable climate may take several years, even with the most competent of top managements. The negative effects of a deep-seated adverse managerial climate are difficult to reverse. The effects on sales and profits can be disastrous.

Although somewhat oversimplified, the cost-reduction sequence described above illustrates the impact upon climate over time. Unfortunately, top management typically does not become fully aware of worsening trends in managerial climate until those trends are manifested in falling productivity or sharply declining profits. By then, the damage may be so severe that it at best requires extensive corrective action, or at worst is irreparable. In some instances, the unhealthy trends are never detected or associated with corresponding declines in results. In such cases the outlook is truly ominous. To avoid this sequence of events that lead to serious trouble, management must have valid and accurate information concerning the internal environment, in a form that illuminates trends. With such information available, programs can be implemented more effectively and modified when necessary.

The implementation of any large-scale program is apt to exert important influences on internal organizational processes. To understand the nature of these effects fully, management must follow them over a period of time. A single climate analysis cannot provide complete understanding. Although providing valuable information, it can indicate only what the climate is like at a particular point. It cannot indicate what the climate has been or where it is going. Furthermore, a single climate analysis cannot demonstrate causality. That is, it cannot provide conclusive evidence that the existing climate has resulted from a specific set of circumstances.

For management to test cause and effect, periodic assessments of climate are necessary. Such a strategy enables control over the interval between implementation of a new program and the consequent managerial climate, thereby making a more accurate analysis of causality possible. The next step would be to relate managerial climate to indexes of productivity. In the context of climate analysis, these result measurements can contribute to better planning. On their own, they provide after-the-fact data, not the information necessary for solving or preventing problems.

The frequency of climate surveys depends upon the nature of the organization's unique situation. In times of rapid change, surveys may be required fairly often. In general, companies find it most useful to conduct climate surveys every one to two years.

The experience of a mining firm that conducted climate surveys for four consecutive years underscores the need for an ongoing monitoring process because of the dynamic nature of management. The company found that a systematic program of periodic surveys provided trend data from which critical before-the-fact information could be extrapolated. Armed with such data, management found itself in a position to anticipate potential problems and correct them before they materialized. Top management used the data to develop and implement programs that were attuned to the company's needed priorities. Repeat surveys served as the vehicles for evaluating the effectiveness of newly instituted performance planning and appraisal systems, as well as for assessing modifications to the compensation program. Detailed analyses by level and unit revealed significant improvements in climate, consistent with the company's change efforts.

Translating Issues to Action

The fourth company involved in our comparison of the use of climate results, a hydraulics equipment manufacturer, considered a climate survey to be a first step in helping to focus attention on significant areas of management concern. This company believes that the most effective way to use climate findings is to relate them to their causes.

In one procedure that was formulated to accomplish this goal, consultants interviewed members of top management as a prelude to group meetings at lower levels. After obtaining a thorough understanding of top management's perspective, the consultants led a series of thirteen peer-group meetings involving a total of 144 middle- and lower-level managers. Survey results were presented to the group members, who were in turn asked to describe specific conditions, practices, or incidents that might have produced the findings. The participants were then encouraged to offer their own recommendations for corrective action.

The specific insights gained through this program made it possible to address highly complex climate issues with direct, concrete actions. Within six months, thirty-two specific actions, ranging from streamlining the authorization procedure on capital expenditures to wide dissemination of the company's five-year plans, had been taken. While many of the problems uncovered by the survey were not surprises to management, the process of follow-up action proved to be the needed impetus for change.

The experience of the hydraulics equipment manufacturer illustrates how dissemination of climate information can be an important management tool, especially for opening up communications around sensitive issues that have remained unspoken problems for some time. In addition, dissemination and response provide an excellent method of increasing trust and confidence in the competence of management and workers. Cooperating on the solution of a problem is the best way to develop good rapport and a sense of mutual reliance. The resolution of problems in this way strengthens an organization's development as a results-oriented, effective enterprise.

The four companies, although utilizing distinct approaches to applying climate findings, did follow in one way or another most of the basic guidelines for improving organizational climate. The ultimate goals of each approach were to delineate problems as precisely as possible and commit management to planning for their solution. In each, representatives report that significant progress has been made, both in improving the management climate and in organizational performance.

Options for Management

Although specific objectives vary among organizations and climate analysis investigates a broad variety of issues, four basic categories of actions are open to management. While the number of policy changes, new programs, alternate methods, and other factors that can be introduced are limitless, they all relate to strategy and planning, organization structure, management processes, or human resources.

Strategy and Planning

A plan can be easily modified. As the survey results are examined, they often point to needed changes in goals, objectives, or strategies. Is appropriate, timely information available for setting goals and making decisions? Is the organization responsive to its external environment? Has sufficient attention been paid to the long-range developments, or has the organization limited itself to dealing with immediate challenges? Finally, are the strategies, plans, and decisions clearly understood by those who must implement them? At times, it is the strategies themselves that are brought into question through a climate study; at others, it is the plans to implement those strategies. In either case, management can take direct action to correct deficiencies.

Organizational Structure

The climate study often points to structural elements that would benefit from specific change. Do the results indicate that the structure facilitates or hinders the flow of information, decision-making, and coordination of efforts among units? Do business units have sufficient resources to focus on their objectives? Do related units operate synergistically or in competition with one another? Are there effective channels for upward, downward, and lateral communications?

Management Processes

Management can make substantial changes in the processes by which the company is managed. Is delegation broad, on a results-only basis, or are people expected to follow a path that has been carefully laid out for them? Does the compensation system support corporate direction, or is it merely a method for distributing funds in a way that minimizes dissatisfaction? Is accountability sharp enough to identify failure, or so diffuse as to be useless as a management tool? These management processes can all be changed in ways that will have dramatic impact on the climate.

Human Resources

Finally, does the organization have a wealth of the right talents? Are people being appropriately developed for current and future positions? Are they motivated and committed to the purposes of the organization? Change in people can take one of two directions, development or replacement. Rarely does an organization take one of these paths to the exclusion of the other. Management must be attuned to the degree to which each will contribute to the organization's health.

Climate Analysis—the Management Tool of the Future

Climate analysis is one of the most significant management techniques to be developed in the past twenty-five years—the one that speaks to the challenges facing American business today and in the forseeable future. At a time when government regulation and societal pressures have severely constrained the actions that management can take, it becomes critically important that the management resources throughout an organization should be maximally effective in developing and applying new solutions to fit new problems.

More and more, productivity is becoming the key to business success. Using the results of climate analysis—a form of data not available in the past—top management is in a position to create an internal environment that stimulates the motivations and talents of those within the organization to focus the "right" actions on the "right" issues to achieve the organization's major objectives.

Notes

1. F.C. Mann, "Studying and Creating Change: A Means to Understanding Social Organization," in *Research in Industrial Human Relations* (Madison, Wis.: Industrial Relations Research Association, 1957), pp. 146-167.

2. Nancy Morse and E. Reimer, "The Experimental Change of a Major Organizational Variable," *Journal of Abnormal and Social Psychology* 52 (1956):120-129.

Appendix A
A Word About
Causality

Throughout this book we describe relationships between two phenomena, both measured at the same point in time. Such measurements do not establish causality, since A could cause B, B could cause A, or both could be caused by C. Our basic thesis is that changes in climate cause changes in organizational outcomes. Laboratory studies where conditions can be controlled clearly demonstrate this phenomenon, and we have described one such study in chapter 2. In the real world of operating companies, the controls necessary to "prove" causality are difficult to establish. We could cite dozens of instances in which companies took specific actions based on a climate analysis and experienced dramatic rises both in sales and profitability and in climate scores. Such citations would offer no more scientific proof than do the correlations we offer in chapter 8 between climate measures and five-year growth in profitability. At this point, the reader must judge for himself whether the weight of evidence supports the hypothesis that climate causes performance.

Appendix B
Items Included in Each
of the Climate
Dimensions

ORGANIZATIONAL CLARITY

To what extent do goals provide a useful context for the everyday functioning of this organization?

To what extent does this organization have clear goals?

Planning for the achievement of goals in this organization tends to be formal.

Planning for the achievement of goals in this organization tends to be complete.

Planning for the achievement of goals in this organization tends to be oriented toward the long term.

Decision making in this organization tends to be based on a long-range view.

To what extent does this organization have defined plans to meet its goals?

DECISION MAKING STRUCTURE

To what extent does the current reporting structure facilitate or hinder implementation of the organization's strategies?

To what extent does the current reporting structure facilitate or hinder the achievement of the organization goals?

To what extent do the systems in this organization provide a manager with the information he needs for decision making?

To what extent are decisions in this organization based on adequate information?

To what extent does the current reporting structure facilitate or hinder coordination of efforts?

ORGANIZATIONAL INTEGRATION

To what extent do the various units in this organization understand each other's problems and difficulties?

Communications laterally to you from others at the same organizational levels tend to be extremely good.

Everything considered, communications in this organization tend to be extremely good.

How clear are managers concerning the interrelationships of their own jobs with those of others?

To what extent do the various units in this organization understand each other's objectives and goals?

To what extent do various units in this organization truly cooperate with one another?

To what extent do you feel that you are sufficiently aware of things that are happening in other areas of the organization which might have an effect on how you do your job?

MANAGEMENT STYLE

To what extent are people in this organization free to take independent actions that are necessary to carry out their job responsibilities?

To what extent are managers encouraged to take reasonable risks in their efforts to increase the effectiveness of this organization?

To what extent is open discussion of conflicts encouraged?

177

To what extent are managers encouraged to innovate in their jobs?

To what extent is constructive criticism encouraged within this organization?

Communications downward to you from above tend to be extremely good.

To what extent do managers receive the support they need from higher levels of management to successfully carry through their job responsibilities?

PERFORMANCE ORIENTATION

To what extent are managers held personally accountable for the end results they produce or fail to produce?

The measures or yardsticks used to judge managerial performance in this organization tend to be very clear.

To what extent are managers within this organization expected to meet demands for high levels of performance?

To what extent are the goals in this organization truly challenging?

How clear are managers about the end results that are expected of them in their jobs?

ORGANIZATIONAL VITALITY

To what extent is this organization responsive to changes in its business environment?

Goals in this organization tend to be venturesome.

Decision making in this organization tends to be innovative.

Decision making in this organization tends to be timely.

Relative to its competition, this organization is a pacesetter.

What is your estimate of the overall vitality of this organization as reflected by such things as a sense of urgency and a rapid pace of activities?

COMPENSATION

To what extent are managers in this organization offered benefits which are competitive with similar organizations?

Considering the work you do, how satisfactory is your present compensation?

To what extent is your pay high compared to others in this organization with similar responsibilities?

To what extent is your pay high compared to people in other organizations with similar responsibilities?

The relationship in this organization between compensation and individual performance tends to be very strong.

HUMAN RESOURCE DEVELOPMENT

Overall, how would you rate the opportunities for promotion within the organization?

When a management vacancy exists, the search within the organization to fill that vacancy tends to be very broad.

How successful is this organization in developing people from within for bigger jobs?

To what extent does this organization provide opportunities for individual growth and development?

To what extent does your job present a significant challenge to you?

To what extent are the talents of managers appropriately matched to the demands of their job?

* Items have been slightly reworded to account for the response scales.

Index

Index

Accountability: assessment of, 7, 8, 52, 158, 173; and demand and satisfaction, 65-66, 77-78; of human resource (personnel) executive, 165; MBO and, 157-158; as motivation, 144-145; organizational structure and, 35, 59, 128, 149; for performance, 28, 29, 38. *See also* Performance orientation

Action-oriented approach, 70, 166-167, 172

"Agency" (federal): restructuring of, 112-115

Ajax Products, 6, 7-9, 10

Alpha Corporation, 42-53, 55

American Distributing (organization), 147-152

American Tobacco Company, 3

Attitude surveys: vs. climate analysis, 9-10

Banking: action-oriented approach in, 166-167; attitudes toward automation of, 162-164; decision-making in, 71

Bluestone Mining Corporation, 121-126, 129

Brown & Williamson Tobacco Corporation, 3

Burlingham Engine Company, 159-164

Business: development, stages of, 80-84; strategy and planning, 87-101, 173. *See also* Organization

Capital intensity, 37, 79-80

Career development. *See* Human resources

Cargo Shipping Company, 87-91, 95, 98

Causality, 171, 175

Change: acceptance of, 157; assessment of, over time, 169-171; commitment to, 168-169; in manpower development, 148-150; resistance to, 153. *See also* Innovation

Chief Executive Officer, The (Rock), 6

Clerical Equipment Company, 115-119

Climate, management: antecedents of, 11-15; complexity of, 10; consistency of, within organization, 61-63; defined, 4-5, 25; demand, 64-67; dimensions (*see* Climate measurement); intended, 14, 15, 17-18, 19, 33-34; issues, MBO and, 154-157; nature of, 4-5; ratings, organizational differences and, 67-70; and results, 63-64; "right," 61-84; role of, 3-10; trends, within organization, 55-60; weaknesses, 6

Climate analysis: by Ajax Products, 7-9; attitude surveys vs., 9-10; and causality, 171, 175; and communication, 20-21; of external climate, 159; by IH, 6-7; perception in, 17, 26-27, 51-52, 55, 57, 58; and performance objectives, 126; role of, in manpower development, 150-152; and structural problems, 103-119; as tool, 5, 10, 70, 140, 147, 168, 172, 174

Climate measurement: approach to, 27-29; eight dimensions in, 29-32, 33-40, 41, 71; and monitoring climate over time, 169-171; response to, 165-174; standard survey form in, 28-32; survey results interpreted, 33-40, 41-53, 55-60, 65-79, 88-101, 104-111, 113-115, 117-119, 123-145, 148-152, 155-158, 160-164, 165, 166-174; two perspectives of, 25-27

Communication: of compensation policy, 39; downward, 15, 35, 50, 170; failure/limitation of, 34, 35,

Communication (cont.)
   39, 50, 125, 170; of intended climate, 17-18, 19, 33-34; interunit,
   36; and motivation, 17-21, 50;
   organization size and, 79; of survey
   results, 165-166, 169, 170; upward,
   19-20, 21, 47, 128, 170. *See also*
   Organizational integration
Company profiles: Alpha, 42-53, 55;
   American Distributing, 147-152;
   Burlingham Engine Company, 159-
   164; Cargo Shipping Company, 87-
   Company, 115-119; Comparisons
   of, 55-60, 61-63, 67-78, 87-101,
   121-145; Driver Corporation, 103-
   112; Equipment Manufacturing
   Company, 87, 91-95; Magnum
   Foods Company, 87, 98-101; Thermal Gas Company, 87, 95-98; within organization, 55-60; Zenith Distributing, 154-157
Compensation. *See* Pay practices

Decision-making: and action-oriented
   problem-solving, 166-167; as climate dimension, 29, 34-35, 78;
   communication and, 82, 170; delegation of, 46, 51-52, 79; organizational, 46, 66, 79, 82, 94, 170, 177;
   perception of, 34-35, 39, 46, 48-49,
   51-52, 71, 94; "timeliness" of, 48-
   49. *See also* Leadership
Demand, 64-67, 77-78. *See also* Accountability; Human resources
Depression, the, 13, 147
Driver Corporation, 103-112
Dun's Review, 4

Economic environment, 11, 12, 13
Environment: external, 11-13, 159-
   164; work, demand and satisfaction
   in, 14, 65-67, 77-78
Equipment Manufacturing Company,
   87, 91-95
External forces and influences, 11-13,
   159-164

Factor analysis: defined, 28
Financial World, 4

Government, 11, 12-13

Hawthorne studies, 9
Hay Associates, 27; and Hay Management Climate Survey, 28
Hazlitt Corporation, 121, 135-140
History, organizational, 13
Human resources, 173-174; and accountability for climate, 165; and
   concern for people, 74; and human
   resource development, 29, 40, 50,
   52-53, 178; and job security, 12,
   75-78, 90, 128-129, 140; manpower development, 147-152; and
   perception of opportunity, 29, 40,
   50, 52-53, 150. *See also* Accountability; Perception

Incentives. *See* Motivation
Industry profiles. *See* Company profiles
Innovation, 12; and compensation/
   reward, 123, 126-129; leadership
   style and, 14-15, 80, 95, 117; and
   resistance to change, 153; and risk-
   taking, 38, 69, 127, 131. *See also*
   Change; Decision-making
Insurance industry: profiles of, 71,
   121, 129-133, 135
International Harvester Company, 6-7,
   10

Job security, 12, 75-78, 90, 128-129,
   140. *See also* Human resources

Kelly-Landor Corporation, 121, 133-
   135
Kingsley Insurance Company, 121,
   129-133, 135

Leadership: and delegation of authority, 36-37, 47, 57, 78; differing
   styles of, 14-15, 79-80; dominant

force of, 15; and management style
as climate dimension, 14, 29, 36-
37, 47, 57, 63, 69-70, 78, 123,
177-178; and management style
related to results, 63; and management style as two-way process, 37;
and motivation, 14, 18, 141-144.
See also Decision-making
Liggett & Myers Tobacco Company, 3
Line unit: defined, 58; and staff-line
differences, 57-60
Lorillard, P., Company, 3, 4

McCormick, Brooks, 6
Magnum Foods Company, 87, 98-101
Management: by objectives (MBO),
153-158; climate (*see* Climate, management); options for, 172-174;
processes, changes in, 173; results-
oriented, 38, 148-152, 153-158;
role of, 13-15; style (*see* Leadership)
Management Climate Survey, 28-32
Manpower development, 147-152. *See
also* Human resources
Manufacturing industry profiles. *See*
Company profiles
Market environment, 11, 12, 13
Maslow, Abraham, 143
Morale: compensation and, 52; demand, 64-67. *See also* Accountability; Human resources; Motivation; Perception
Motivation: accountability as, 144-
145; communication and, 17-21,
50; defined, 18, 25; by "hierarchy
of internal needs," 143; incentive
programs, 7, 121-145; of key staff
managers, 141-144; leadership and,
14, 18, 141-144; MBO and, 153-
154, 157; and perception, 18-19,
25; rewards and, 7, 20, 121-145;
and security vs. risk, 89-90; and use
of titles, 145. *See also* Accountability; Pay practices

Opportunity: perception of, 29, 40,
50, 52-53, 150. *See also* Human
resources; Perception
Options for management, 172-174
Organization: assessment matrix, 82-
84; climate relationships within,
61-63; perception of, by outside
world, 159; performance by, 154-
157; size, 79. *See also* Business;
Performance orientation; Productivity
Organizational clarity: as climate
dimension, 29, 33-34, 45-46, 73,
128; and line-staff difference, 58-
59; and performance, 63
Organizational differences: and climate ratings (compared), 67-70
Organizational history, 13
Organizational integration: as climate
dimension, 29, 35-36, 46-47, 73,
84, 177; and conflict, 94; and performance, 63. *See also* Communication
Organizational restructuring, 103-119,
173; MBO and, 153-158
Organizational vitality: as climate
dimension, 29, 48-49, 53, 178;
perception of, 38-39. *See also* Decision-making; Leadership

Pay practices: actual vs. perceived, 20,
52, and compensation as climate
dimension, 29, 39, 49, 52, 63, 122-
125, 178; and compensation/incen-
tive programs, 121-130, 135, 138-
139, 145; IH reward system, 7;
related to performance, 29, 39, 49,
59, 63, 68. *See also* Motivation
Perception: of benefits, 133-135; in
climate analysis, 17, 26-27, 51-52,
55, 57, 58; of decision-making process, 34-35, 39, 46, 48-49, 51-52,
71, 94; of job security, 75-78; by
management, 153; and motivation,
18-19, 25, 133-135; of opportunity, 29, 40, 50, 52-53, 150; of

Perception (cont.)
    organization, by outside world,
    159; organizational clarity and, 29,
    33-34, 45-46, 58, 59, 63, 73, 128,
    177; of organizational vitality, 38-
    39; of pay, 20. *See also* Human
    resources; Motivation; Organiza-
    tional clarity
Performance orientation: as climate
    dimension, 28, 29, 37-38, 48, 58,
    78, 152, 178; demand and, 64-67;
    and results, 63. *See also* Account-
    ability; Results
Personnel. *See* Human resources
Philip Morris, Inc., 3, 4
P. Lorillard Company, 3, 4
Porter, Lyman, 143
Problem-solving: action oriented, 166-
    167. *See also* Decision-making
Productivity: falling, as manifestation
    of trend, 171; managerial, impact
    of, 9; measure of, 155; morale and,
    64-65; rate of increase of, 170. *See
    also* Performance orientation
Profiles. *See* Company profiles
Profit-climate relationships, 63-64

Reader's Digest, 4
Relationships: climate, among organi-
    zations, 61-63; and communication,
    19; of compensation and perfor-
    mance, 29, 39, 49, 59, 63, 68; and
    interrelations of individuals, 153; of
    management climate and organiza-
    tional performance, 154-157, 175
Results: climate and, 63-64; interpre-
    tation of (*see* Climate measure-
    ment); by management levels, 55-
    56; by organizational units, 56-57;
    and results-oriented management,
    38, 148-152, 153-158. *See also*
    Accountability; Performance orien-
    tation

Retail businesses, restaurants, and
    hotels: profiles of, 71-73
Reynolds, R.J., Tobacco Company, 3,
    4
Risk: vs. job security, 12, 75-78, 90,
    128-129, 140. *See also* Human re-
    sources; Innovation
Rock, Robert: *The Chief Executive
    Officer,* 6

Security. *See* Risk
Social environment, 11-12, 13
Spencer-Huxley Company, 121, 126-
    129
Staff: -line differences, 57-60; man-
    agers, key, 141-144; units defined,
    58. *See also* Leadership
Strategy and planning, 10, 87-101,
    173
Success: climate and, 5-9; typical ex-
    planations of, 3-4
Survey Research Center (University of
    Michigan), 28

Technological environment, 11, 12
Thermal Gas Company, 87, 95-98
Tobacco industry, 3-4, 9
Tradition, company, 13

United Diversity Corporation, 121,
    141-145
University of Michigan, 28
Utilities industry: profiles of, 71, 72-
    75, 76, 95-98

Weisman, George, 4

Yellen, Manuel, 4

Zenith Distributing (organization),
    154-157

About the Authors

George G. Gordon, who holds a doctorate in psychology from Purdue University, has spent his career as both an internal and an external consultant to a wide variety of business and nonprofit organizations. As president of the Research for Management Division of Hay Associates, he is currently responsible for a broad program of activities focused on managerial effectiveness.

Walter M. Cummins, a novelist and story writer, chairs the English Department on the Florham-Madison campus of Fairleigh Dickinson University. He has participated in the development and implementation of programs in technical and organizational communication.